Praise for Jodie Eckleberry-Hunt's

GETTING TO GOOD RIDDANCE

"Real from cover to cover. A rarity to find a resource to provide clients that is rooted in the science of behavior, provides intentional self-compassion, and a bonus a spoonful of profanity needed to take the edge off and get to the business of healing. This is a gem, funny to the bone."

—Nicole R. Najar, PsyD, ABPP,
Clinical Health Psychologist

"After a breakup, you probably need a motivational coach, a foul-mouthed best friend, and a wise sage who can guide you in the right direction. In *Getting to Good Riddance*, Jodie Eckleberry-Hunt gives you all three . . . Filled with practical strategies, wisdom from psychological research, and questions to prompt deep personal growth, this book is exactly what you need to create more satisfying relationships."

—Lisa Williams LCSW, host of *Self Help Bookshelf* podcast

"*Getting to Good Riddance* is a perfect balance of humor, case studies, science, and profanity! . . . This book is relevant to so many situations other than romantic breakup—leaving unhealthy friendships, setting family boundaries, work relationships, and most importantly how to be more self-aware to take good self-care. Dr. Eckleberry-Hunt gives you the skills to own your own shitshow and create the life you want!"

—Jenny Williams, OT, owner of
Innovative Occupational Therapy Solutions

"Dr. Eckleberry-Hunt loads *Getting to Good Riddance* with actionable, practical advice that will help you move through and beyond a tough breakup . . . As a divorce attorney and mediator for over two decades,

I highly recommend this quick read for anyone struggling with the intense pain of breaking up. One day at a time with forward momentum is the only way. And when a day is too much, a moment. You can survive, and with this book, you can also thrive."

—Gabrielle Hartley, Esq., author of
Better Apart: The Radically Positive Way to Separate, founder of The Better Apart Method

"Long awaited and overdue. This is the book to guide one through the emotional roller coaster of a relationship breakup and to come out whole on the other side. Written with wisdom and straight-talk, based on scientifically proven coping strategies, Dr. Eckleberry-Hunt enlightens us with wit, spicy humor, compassion and self-revelation . . . It instills hope and promise that 'getting to good riddance' is not an end but rather a new beginning."

—Anne Van Dyke, PhD, ABPP,
Health Psychologist, Telebehavioral Health Therapist

"If you're struggling to get over a breakup, and you're having trouble seeing the light at the end of the tunnel, this book is for you."

—*Tri-County Times*

"Jodie Eckleberry-Hunt presents a compassionate, realistic, hopeful, humorous explanation of the process of working through the grief to get through a breakup . . . She covers it all from what went wrong, what I contributed, what I ignored, how I can grow from this."

—Ruth M. Shoemaker, PhD,
Licensed Clinical Psychologist,
founder of Anchor Psychology Center

"*Getting to Good Riddance* takes you through the breakup journey, starting with the stages of grief and self-doubt to the possibility of acceptance, gratitude, and hope. Despite the pain, you will learn to use humor and some profanity to keep you out of the fantasy world and in the reality of true closure and moving on . . . This book is practical and will help you move out of loneliness and despair and hopefully propel you to find self-love, happiness, and the strength to build a better life."

—Lori Washe, MD, medical director and physician Premier Private Physicians in Troy, Michigan, faculty member Oakland University William Beaumont Medical School

"*Getting to Good Riddance* transcends romantic relationships and is applicable for friendships, family, and work relationships . . . This book gave me the good feels, and by the end, I felt the author was my personal positive self-talk coach (foul-mouthed, yet uplifting). For anyone, regardless of current Facebook relationship status, I couldn't provide a stronger recommendation!"

—Kelley Williams, MD

"Eckleberry-Hunt's book proves salient for anyone who has suffered a loss (even the non-romantic ones). Her writing creates the feel of a meeting over coffee and conversation with a highly trained (and humorous) psychologist who uses scientific methods to take you to places you dare to venture . . . Eckleberry-Hunt wraps you in a warm, cozy blanket while safely taking you to vulnerable spaces. She makes it easy to imagine a new reality! I highly recommend this book to all who have suffered a loss of any kind."

—Kristi Jo Wilson, PhD, RN, MSN, FNP-BC, CAFCI

"*Getting to Good Riddance* is a complete guidebook to get you through the breakup and life beyond. It is a thorough resource to utilize when your life gets flipped upside down and you are stuck on how to move forward . . . This book has answers, guidance, and if you have the courage, a way forward to a better version of you."

—Amy Bray, LMSW

"Navigating a breakup is like traveling through an emotional shit storm filled with traps, hazards, and detours. *Getting to Good Riddance* will help you identify the emotional storm you are in and warn you of traps, hazards, and detours along the way—allowing you to find your way to the other side where you can create your own pathway to happiness and contentment."

—Britt A. Nielsen, PsyD, ABPP,
MetroHealth Medical Center

"A record-breaking snowstorm stranded me and my girlfriend at our high school for two days. After a few hours of being trapped, my girlfriend broke up with me, and there was nowhere to go. It was brutal. If only I had access to *Getting to Good Riddance* at that tender young age to navigate the emotional debris."

—Garry Meier, host of *The Garry Meier Show*

"Dr. Eckleberry-Hunt is a maestro of teaching us how to let go of relationships that are over and move on to something better. You won't regret picking up this book for yourself or someone you care about who is struggling with a relationship's end."

—Heather Kirkpatrick, PhD, Licensed Psychologist

"Dr. Eckleberry-Hunt delivers again with a book full of practical and impactful ways to navigate the breakup process. Her unique blend of irreverence and empathy is engaging from the first page to the last . . . Striking a good balance between a strong clinical foundation and relatable examples, *Getting to Good Riddance* should be required reading for anyone facing the end of a relationship."

—Darren Jones, PhD, LP,
Chief of Behavioral Health, Beaumont Health System

GETTING TO
GOOD RIDDANCE

ALSO BY JODIE ECKLEBERRY-HUNT

Move on Motherf*cker:
Live, Laugh & Let Sh*t Go

GETTING TO
GOOD RIDDANCE

| *A No-Bullsh*t Breakup Survival Guide* |

. . .

Jodie Eckleberry-Hunt, Ph.D., A.B.P.P.

TURNER
PUBLISHING COMPANY

Turner Publishing Company
Nashville, Tennessee
www.turnerpublishing.com

Cover design by Grace Cavalier
Book design by Anna B. Knighton

Library of Congress Cataloging-in-Publication Data
Names: Eickleberry-Hunt, Jodie, author.
Title: Getting to good riddance : a breakup survival guide /
by Jodie Eickleberry-Hunt, Ph.D., A.B.P.P.
Description: Nashville, Tennessee : Turner Publishing
Company, [2022] | Includes bibliographical references. |
Identifiers: LCCN 2021039679 (print) | LCCN 2021039680 (ebook) |
ISBN 9781684428489 (paperback) | ISBN 9781684428496 (hardcover) |
ISBN 9781684428502 (ebook)
Subjects: LCSH: Man-woman relationships—Psychological aspects. |
Separation (Psychology) | Interpersonal relations.
Classification: LCC HQ801 .E37 2022 (print) |
LCC HQ801 (ebook) | DDC 306.7—dc23
LC record available at https://lccn.loc.gov/2021039679
LC ebook record available at https://lccn.loc.gov/2021039680

Printed in the United States of America

Table of Contents

Foreword

BY ANNE DOHRENWEND, PHD, ABPP

Imagine two children waiting in the rain for a school bus. The bus approaches, hits a puddle, and splashes both children, leaving them covered in muddy water. One child begins to cry, exclaiming, "He did that on purpose!" The other child laughs and pumps the air with his fist: "Excellent! I get out of math class!" The same event results in two, diametrically opposed reactions. How can this be? Because the event occurred to two different people. Though both children were exposed to the same experience, getting splashed by a bus, their personal interpretations or thoughts resulted very different emotional consequences.

The idea that thoughts create feelings has been around for a long time. Even Shakespeare notes the connection between thoughts and feelings. When Hamlet describes Denmark as a "prison," his friends, Guildenstern and Rosencrantz object. After all, to these friends, Hamlet is a prince living an entitled life of luxury in court. Keen on human nature, Hamlet acknowledges that one person's life of luxury can be another person's prison. It is all a matter of perception and one's perception is shaped by one's thoughts. "Why then 'tis none to you; for there is nothing either good or bad, but thinking makes it so. To me it is a prison."

Like Hamlet, many of us are trapped in prisons of our own making. This is not to say that all suffering is self-inflicted. With life, there is suffering. The loss of loved ones, injustice, and poverty result in suffering. Illness and pain result in suffering. That said, the same event will impact individuals differently depending upon their beliefs and thoughts about that event. Suffering can be amplified or reduced by perception. In some cases, even benign events can be perceived in such a way as to create prisons of misery. While psychologists cannot eliminate pain from their clients' lives, they can help clients minimize unnecessary suffering by finding the key to self-imposed suffering, thus freeing them to experience greater happiness.

As a psychologist, I have seen a great deal of unnecessary suffering: LGBT patients suffering from terrible beliefs about themselves due to internalized homophobia; victims of sexual assault struggling with self-blame and shame; people who tell themselves they are unlovable or that all people are untrustworthy. There is always a foundation upon which the walls of the prison are built—a father with serial infidelity or an abusive, critical parent. Early experiences like these can create a foundation for a flawed or distorted belief system, which parlays into negative thinking that follows an individual for the rest of their life. Correcting distorted thinking can be the key to finding peace and happiness.

The way we think about and interpret events in our lives has emotional consequences, and it has behavioral consequences as well. The boy who tells himself that the bus driver intentionally splashed him with mud will likely feel enraged and perhaps sad. He will also probably act differently toward the bus driver when he boards the bus the next day. Maybe he will give him the beady eye or refuse to respond to the bus driver's friendly greeting. The bus driver, feeling the sting of the boy's behavior toward him, may stop engaging with the boy altogether. The bus driver's failure to greet him in the same way he greets the other children would only serve to reinforce the boy's initial belief that the bus driver is out to get him, resulting in more of the same negative emotional consequences. If the boy goes on to put a negative spin on neutral events, he is likely to begin to adopt a belief that people are untrustworthy and unkind. He will be able to point to the experience with the bus driver as just one example in a long line of similarly negative interactions with people throughout his life . . . and so, the prison of misery is laid, brick by brick, formed from negative thinking and its consequences, emotional and behavioral. How do we escape from unnecessary suffering? We learn to change our thinking. We attack our negative thoughts with every ounce of will, replacing negative thoughts with helpful, "rational," thinking.

The word "rational" is key. Cognitive-behavioral therapy is not about whitewashing the truth. It is a therapy that focuses on replacing irrationally negative thoughts with balanced, rational thoughts with the understanding that balanced, rational thoughts will result in better emotional consequences and, subsequently, more functional behavior. It is not necessary for the unhappy boy in the bus scenario to love getting splashed by the bus to avoid misery. To avoid misery, he need only replace his overly negative belief with a balanced, rational belief. After all, there is no evidence that the bus driver splashed him on purpose. If the boy simply interrupts this negative interpretation and replaces it with a more balanced interpretation, he will feel better. For instance, he could replace "he did that on purpose" with "bummer, I was so geeked to wear my new shirt to school and now I have to change. I'm disappointed, but I can wear it tomorrow." This new way of thinking about being splashed results in a different emotional consequence, one of disappointment and mild irritation rather than rage. His subsequent behavior with the bus driver will be different as well. The boy might not think the bus driver is the most attentive driver. He may even give the bus a wide berth on future rainy days, but it is less likely that the boy will convey distain when the bus driver next welcomes him aboard.

Imagine that. We can put an end to needless suffering simply by changing the way we think! It sounds easy enough. Why do we need books to help us? Let's face it, cognitive therapy is not rocket science. Look for irrational, negative thoughts that result in lousy emotional consequences, interrupt those negative thoughts, replace them with rational, balanced thoughts, and experience better emotional consequences.

Simple enough, only it isn't.

For one thing, you might have a hard time identifying your negative thoughts. In fact, you might vigorously defend them. You might have difficulty identifying balanced replacement thoughts because you have no practice. You've only practiced negative thoughts. An underlying trauma, an event that created the foundation of your prison walls, may remained buried and out of sight. To make change stick, we need to see the foundations of our beliefs; we need insight. Insight both motivates and permits change. So, changing negative thoughts is not as easy as it may seem. It takes practice, determination, and insight.

Now, what does all this have to do with ending a crappy relationship? Many times, shitty thinking is the problem. (Wow, it's fun to swear!) Shitty thinking often plays a role in selecting a problem partner in the first place, and shitty thinking often plays a role in the choice to remain in a bad relationship. What greater prison is there than the prison of living with someone you don't love or who mistreats you? What greater misery than to sleep, eat, and spend each precious day of life with someone who is unkind?

Often, the bad relationship is obviously bad. Friends see it. Family sees it. Even the individuals in the relationship know that the relationship is flawed, yet they feel stuck and unable to end it. People in bad relationships usually have thoughts that keep them stuck, and some of these thoughts fall into the category of negative thinking. As a psychologist, I have heard all sorts of thoughts for staying in bad relationships that make no sense. Here are a few: "He loses his temper, but his father was worse."

"All relationships are hard." "I won't find anyone better." Sometimes, self-talk can occur at the unconscious level. "I deserve to be treated this way." "I am unlovable." "I can make her love me." "If he loves me, he will stop drinking."

It takes work to gain insight and to challenge unhelpful thoughts that lead to sticking with relationships that are, frankly, better off ended. In *Getting to Good Riddance*, Dr. Eckleberry-Hunt takes on negative self-talk that inhibits breaking up with an ill-matched or lousy partner. She does so with warmth and humor and a ~~heck~~ hell of lot of swearing. Her book, and her previous work, *Move on Mother F*ucker*, offer an easy-to-understand approach to cognitive therapy. Moreover, Dr. Eckleberry-Hunt makes use of cursing to add weight behind the punch of thought-stopping.

Thought-stopping, interrupting irrational thoughts, has been around for a long time. So has swearing! In the 1960s, Albert Ellis told his clients to stop "shoulding on yourself" and to quit "musterbating." Even back then, swearing was encouraged to "fucking stop!" that shitty thinking. Swearing works for many reasons; I'll leave it to Dr. Eckleberry-Hunt to explain why swearing is like dynamite to negative thinking. I will say this: swearing adds fun fury and makes us feel in charge. When people are stuck in a crappy relationship, they often don't feel in charge of their own choices, and they often stop experiencing the healing power of humor.

Of course, there is more to ending a shitty relationship than interrupting negative thoughts. As intimated above, individuals stuck in soul-sucking relationships usually have a deep foundation of unhelpful and untrue beliefs that support those negative thoughts. Unearthing crazy beliefs about self-in-relationship makes it easier to buy into busting up the negative thoughts those lousy beliefs create. For instance, if an individual unearths a belief that she is unlovable and discovers that it was planted in her unconscious mind by an inept, traumatized parent, she will be less likely to have the negative thought—"I am unlovable"—and find it easier to identify and counter this negative thought when it arises. Insight picks away at the foundation of the prison walls of negative thinking.

While gaining insight is crucial to ending a bad relationship, improving one's understanding of healthy relationship can ensure a bright future with a warm and loving partner. Dr. Eckleberry-Hunt does a terrific job at identifying the bad characters that engage in abuse. She encourages the reader to unearth unhelpful belief systems and behaviors that open the gate to bad characters, and she offers a path to creating a new foundation of beliefs—one that will open the gate only to loving partners.

For those who have never experienced a healthy, loving relationship, it is hard to tell the difference between love and other emotions that give rise to arousal, excitement, and intensity. If someone's first objects of love, one's parents, were incapable of healthy love, it will take work to root out false beliefs about love and replace those false beliefs with true beliefs. What are some of those true beliefs? Love is not controlling. It is not cruel. It is not selfish. Love may not always be exciting; it may temper with age. Love feels calm and safe. Everyone deserves love- you can belief it!

Love is worth every effort, every bit of work that it may take to obtain. My advice: Never settle for anything short of love. Never settle for anyone who is unloving.

Introduction

Jorge and Lana were in love. It was the kind of love that makes others want to puke. They had sweet names for each other. They couldn't keep their hands off one another. They'd dated eight months and were talking about a future together.

Then, out of the blue, Jorge told Lana it was "over." He had been "lying" to himself. He wasn't really in love. He thought it was best if they ended it. No, they couldn't be friends. There was no need to talk it out. It was seriously over.

Lana was beyond devastated. She was incapacitated. The pain was searing to her core. For Lana, even getting out of bed felt like an overly ambitious goal. She replayed scenes of their relationship over and over in an endless loop, ruminating about what she had done wrong and what was wrong with her. Nothing made sense. She kept coming back to this conclusion: *I'm unlovable. I'm a bad person. I will always be alone. No one wants me. Jorge was the most wonderful, special, incredible guy. I'll never find happiness again. Things will never get better. My life is over.* She was overwhelmed with feelings of despair, hopelessness, fear, hurt, and shame.

I've seen folks like Lana many times over the years. Sometimes they are men, sometimes women. Admittedly, I have not knowingly worked with trans individuals, but I am sure that the feelings of hopelessness and despair after a breakup are universal to all genders, whether in heterosexual, same-sex, or non-binary relationships. The feelings are human.

Of all the types of pain I've seen in the therapy room, it seems that nothing is quite as paralytic as an unwanted breakup. Coping with a death is also incredibly traumatic, but here's the difference: when someone dies, they aren't choosing to reject or leave you (unless we are talking about suicide, which is entirely different altogether). When someone breaks up with you, it is very much like a death (the death of the relationship), but the other person is still living. The other person is choosing to live life without you. In death, there is separation, but you may be comforted in telling yourself the other person isn't choosing to be apart from you. Or they're still with you, just on another plane.

Do you see the difference?

I think the reason breakups hurt even more than the death of a loved one is the knowledge that the other person does not want to be with *you* anymore. That thought and the associated feelings are killer personal.

Relationships are all about attachment. Attachment is that invisible emotional bond we develop with others that ties us to them. It isn't necessarily conscious, but it forms over time as we invest of ourselves into relationships. When we form an emotional bond, it is like we join with another person at the heart. When the bond is broken, it is like we are being ripped apart—which is especially painful when we are not doing the ripping—even more so when we aren't expecting it. There is a massive wound that we feel unable to bind. It seems like daily life just keeps breaking the wound open again. It can feel impossible to heal.

This is why I wrote this book. For years, I've listened to breakup stories; and while there are many different themes, the emotional experiences are similar. People want to understand. They want the pain to go away. Sometimes they want me to help them get the relationship back. It is all an attempt to feel better.

If this is you, know you are not alone—not by a long shot.

I want you to know that this book is not about fixing the relationship or getting it back. It's about healing from a breakup. It is about understanding what in the fresh hell just happened, what it means, and how to feel better. This book is about grieving and moving on in a seriously motivational way—a kick-ass, smash-the-shit-out-of-the-pain, moving-on kind of way.

Yeah, I know—I have to contain my enthusiasm, because it can scare people early on. Perhaps you are thinking: *What the fuck are you talking about? I can barely crawl to the bathroom on my own right now.* Or: *My days are consumed with fantasies of revenge.* Maybe this is you: *I'm so fucked in the head that I don't even know how I feel. It changes by the hour.* Whatever you feel, it is normal after a breakup. Feelings run the gamut and often vacillate quickly.

Regardless of your state at this moment, if you are ready to recover from a breakup, this book is for you. This book is for men, for women, and for non-binary folks.

And this book is not just for people whose partner broke up with them. It is also for people who broke off a relationship they wanted but knew wasn't working. Admittedly, the book is geared more toward people who are devastated that a partner left them. However, there are absolutely times when people end a relationship that their heart wanted because their head told them it was time to be done. It hurts regardless.

My dilemma in working with folks who are reeling from a breakup has been finding a good book for them to read. I feel like reading gives people something to do between visits, stimulates self-refection, and gives new insights. Books give people a sense that they are not alone, but I haven't really found a book with the message I want to convey, which is: *You will feel better, one day at a time. We can do this together. There is hope. Here is what you can do—that really works.*

Because that is what people want. They want to feel productive movement toward understanding and healing. These exist in a psychological place I call good riddance.

I find, after hearing train-wreck stories of breakups, that I'm often thinking *good riddance* about the ex-partner. There are times I am even thinking *good riddance, asshole,* but we'll get to that later. I know the person consulting me isn't ready to hear that yet, so I don't say it, but I know they will be ready to hear it eventually.

Don't be fooled, though. This book isn't negative, and it isn't coming from a jaded perspective. It isn't about beating up the ex-partner, and it isn't about blowing smoke up your ass about how blameless you were in what happened. The book is about channeling whatever fight you have left into getting better, and my point is that oftentimes that energy is found in anger. The trick is not getting stuck in anger, but using it to propel yourself forward. *Getting to Good Riddance* is about taking your frustration and anger, and channeling it into forward progress.

I am a positive person. Seriously, I am an optimist. I believe in love: but in order to find the best love, we often have to experience heartbreak along the way. It is a necessary evil in better understanding ourselves and others. Sometimes it's a wakeup call to our own baggage that we can work on packing up and sending off. This book reflects my deep faith in human resilience, recovery, and growth.

In the end, I know you are better off without that person. How can I know this? Well, we are all better off being with people who want to be with us. It is so good to know this now, so you can move on with your life. How lucky you are to have found this out now, rather than later!

Not feeling lucky right now? Understood.

The people who come to see me generally don't feel lucky. They are feeling guilty, unworthy, regretful, sick inside. They are replaying all the events that led up to the breakup and wondering what went wrong and what they could have done differently. They wonder if . . . just maybe . . . there might be a chance of reconciliation.

Even if the ex-partners did some really shitty things, some people who see me feel sorry for the exes and want to help them with the demons that cause the underlying problems. They tell themselves the ex-partners need help.

All of this is somehow less painful than the truth, which will usher in very scary life changes.

I know all this because I have seen it over and over; yet the people who consult me don't know any of it. They are simply afraid.

Getting to Good Riddance is my spin on moving through the process to the place of being done—to the place of moving on: transcendence. And my method of getting to transcendence involves laughter and lots of it, because humor heals.

In so much of what I do, I look for some way to add in spicy humor, because it is such a powerful antidote to pain. When people come to me with that searing, sickening, aching feeling of rejection and hurt from a breakup, they aren't ready for humor. I get that. But they will be, and I hold that as a goal to get there: the day they look back and think *good riddance, asshole*.

And it doesn't even matter if the other person is an asshole or not. Sometimes they are. Sometimes two people interact such that one or both behave like assholes. Sometimes the people are just too different. In the end, it just doesn't matter.

What matters is that you get to a point of feeling better—of moving on with your life, because you are the one reading this book. You are the one trying to make yourself and your life better. You are the only one you can control. What remains is figuring out what the fuck you're going to do with it. Let's start by getting real, getting into the weeds, and *getting to good riddance*.

Here is the layout of the book. In Chapter 1, I start out with a full explanation of Cognitive-Behavioral Therapy (CBT), mindfulness, positive psychology, humor, and profanity. I explain the science behind the techniques and how they work. The chapter will give you the basic skills to manage your roller-coaster thoughts and emotions. In Chapter 2, shit gets real as I transform the knowledge from Chapter 1 into the Move on, Motherfucker

(MOMF) philosophy, because I understand that breakups impair your ability to think straight and get through the day.

Chapter 3 is about basic survival skills. The chapter is focused on managing the pain that comes right after a relationship ends. It is important to develop a plan to manage yourself so you are able to start moving on, motherfucker. Chapter 4 covers the stages of grief so you have a guide about what to expect and can begin to develop some hope that things will get better. Chapter 5 takes a deep dive into what love is and some of the theories behind what we feel in relationships. The goal is to help you understand some of the storylines that have been driving your behaviors and what to expect in relationships long-term.

Chapter 6 is about infidelity, understanding it, and getting over it. Chapter 7 covers specific types of damaged people who seem to impact our lives like a natural disaster does. These include the narcissist, the dependent, the sociopath, the abuser, and the threatener. Chapter 8 is about your boundaries and things you may do that enable others to hurt you. Chapter 9 is when you think you may be addicted to love because you keep going back for more, knowing that it is a shit sandwich. Chapter 10 mercifully is about turning the page to consider a future without as many assholes in it. Sorry, there will always be some assholes, but this chapter is focused on envisioning their sucking in someone else rather than you. Chapter 11 is putting it all together and moving on to your new life, armed with new knowledge and strength.

What makes this book different from a lot of relationship self-help is that I am not just going to throw a bunch of ideas at you, for you to try. No, I am going to explain to you what the techniques are and how they actually work. I strongly believe that this background will give you deeper insight into your motivations and tendencies. It will help you become a better expert on yourself so you are more effective in making long-term change.

Ready for more? Change starts here.

GETTING TO
GOOD RIDDANCE

Psychology 101

This chapter is the foundation for everything that comes next. I start with the basics of how we think, feel, and behave, and then things will get easier to understand. I promise.

CORE BELIEFS

When we are born, half of our personality is already formed, while the other half is shaped by our life experiences in the first eighteen years or so of life. Our personality contains core beliefs about ourselves, the world, and other people. All information flows through these core beliefs—both positive and negative—which you can also think of as biases or filters. The point is that we see everything through these biased filters, so it is important to be aware of what they are. Again, some are genetic (like being an optimist or pessimist), and some are related to life experiences (like messages our parents taught us).

Core beliefs color our life.

Imagine if my family had repeatedly criticized my weight while I was growing up. I might now believe weight and outward appearances are super-important. I might now define myself by how I look. I might now believe I have to look a certain way to be accepted.

On the other hand, let's say I grew up hearing my parents tell me how loved I am. I might have grown up knowing that love isn't earned, but is freely given. I might have learned how to freely express love for others without fear.

Again, both genetics and childhood experiences shape our core beliefs, which are stable biased filters through which we view our lives. Some common problematic core beliefs about relationships include:

- People aren't to be trusted.
- Worth must be earned.
- Emotions are bad.
- Love must be earned.
- Those you love hurt you the most.
- Physical attractiveness is the key to love and acceptance.

SELF-TALK

Core beliefs drive self-talk. Self-talk is our own voice in our head that's constantly chattering. That voice evaluates things as good or bad, comments on our performance, tells us how great or terrible we are, urges us to do certain things, etc. Our biases drive self-talk.

If I'd learned early in life that people I love hurt me, I might view others through a *distrust* belief filter: my self-talk would tell me not to trust others. If I had heard over and over that I was worthless, I might see myself as unworthy because information is being run through the *unworthy* belief filter: my self-talk would tell me that no one could possibly love me.

Things should start to click with you about now. Maybe you're thinking: *Oh, yeah, now I get why I react in certain ways in certain situations . . .*

Here's the rub: you can't go back and rewrite your beliefs or change your genetic wiring. Being aware of your core beliefs and biases is extremely important, because the insight will allow you to catch your tendencies; however, there is no cure. You must keep fighting the good fight of catching the biases, labeling them as problematic, and not reacting to them. Success is becoming aware of your problematic tendencies and working hard to combat them.

Some common types of negative self-talk related to relationships include:

- No one loves me.
- I'm so unattractive.
- I am not worthy of acceptance. People will see through me.
- I can't be happy.
- I should be what the other person wants me to be.
- Bad things always happen to me.
- What if I get hurt?

There are many more types, but you get the idea.

The opposite can also be true. You can have *positive* self-talk. If you see things positively, you'll see the upside of situations first. If you see people as basically good, you'll tend to be more trusting.

This is how it works: If we are thinking positive thoughts (e.g., good shit is about to happen today), we will feel positive emotions (e.g., excitement). If we are thinking negative thoughts (e.g., bad shit is going down today), we will feel negative emotions (e.g., anxious). Our feelings shape our behavior. For example, if I am thinking positive thoughts, perhaps I do good deeds and give compliments. If I am thinking negative thoughts, I eat a carton of low-carb ice cream and have explosive diarrhea.

We all have self-talk, and negative self-talk isn't all bad if helps us deal with real threats in our environment. Our brains are wired to see negative things so we can overcome threats. This is a survival skill. The trick is to identify which negative self-talk is based on real-life facts and which is a product of our own minds. The goal is not to eliminate negative self-talk but to see it, analyze it, and manage it in order to be healthy.

The key to separating the wheat from the chaff begins with monitoring the entire conversation that goes on inside our heads. It is knowing our biases and tendencies so we can manage them to our benefit. Fortunately, there are several effective research-based strategies to regulate negative beliefs and self-talk, including CBT, mindfulness, positive psychology, humor, and profanity. What is central to each of these strategies is the ability to be intentionally self-aware.

Let me tell you more about each of the strategies, and then I will bring them together at the end.

WHAT IS CBT?

In the 1960's, Aaron Beck, M.D.,[1] noted that individuals who have depression and anxiety say overwhelmingly negative things to themselves. Think of chronic, self-defeating negative self-talk as a disorder. Beck developed Cognitive-Behavioral Therapy or CBT to treat the psychological disorders caused by negative self-talk.

Cognitive refers to what we are thinking. *Behavioral* refers to what we do. CBT interventions include both thought- and behavior-based interventions.

Cognitive interventions involve identifying dysfunctional core beliefs and associated negative self-talk, and stopping them by arguing back, using distraction, or using affirmations. CBT interventions have consistently been shown to work for many people; but it takes a lot of practice over the course of the person's lifetime, because negative self-talk never goes away. The goal is for the person to get better at catching and changing self-talk that is unhealthy.

Behavioral interventions come in here. There are times when we just can't get over the nasty things we are saying to ourselves. In those situations, we change what we are doing. For example, we may call a friend to take a walk. We plan positive activities to boost our mood. We journal instead of eating a tray of brownies. We do something other than reviewing the negative thoughts without end. We avoid things that trigger the negative thoughts. We may find that our stressful thoughts will go away because we are distracting ourselves.

CBT is a proven way of systematically identifying thought patterns, understanding how these patterns affect feelings and behaviors, changing those thought patterns, and changing behaviors. The goal is to feel better.

Here are some ways to apply CBT concepts to relationships.

Origins of distorted beliefs and self-talk:

- I worry a lot that no one will ever be faithful to me because I am not enough. I hate how I look. I'm not that smart. My partner can find someone so much better than me. I find myself checking his cell phone and emails on the sly because I want to see if he is cheating. I need to know. It feels wrong, but I can't stop myself.
- I recognize that my dad cheated on my mom the whole time I was growing up. She would take us kids in the car at night to

see if he was where he said he would be. She was obsessed, but she wouldn't leave him. I always hated that. Mom would tell me dad was confused, and she had to win him over. I learned to see relationships as dysfunctional that way. I was always trying to win my dad over, too—like I was afraid he would leave me too. I see that I have always been afraid of being abandoned by men I love, but I also see that I view men as always prone to wandering.

- I can see that those early experiences have fucked up my thinking. I don't know how to stop it, though.

Once I identify distorted beliefs, I can:

- Recognize how my genetics and life history affect my core beliefs and how my core beliefs affect self-talk. I can then see how negative self-talk affects feelings and the problems that flow from those beliefs and thoughts. I may notice consistent patterns of *what-if* thinking. For example, *What if my partner finds someone better? How will I win him back?* I may also notice a lot of *I-can't* statements like *I can't live without him. I can't be alone. I can't change.*

CBT encourages me to ask myself questions like:

- *What is the evidence that what I am saying to myself is true?* I have to *prove* it or entertain the idea that it is self-created torture. If there is actual evidence, I need to ask myself what I need to do about it. If there is no evidence, I am making problems that don't exist.

For example, I ask myself what evidence I have to support my beliefs. Do I know for certain that my boyfriend is cheating? Can I prove I am not able to be alone? Realistically, I can be alone, sure, but I admit it would be miserable. Regardless, is it helpful to think these things?

I can use counterstatements to argue back with the negative things I say to myself.

- Counterstatements are things a good friend might say or the way a friend would give you another way to look at your situation. For example: *Your thoughts are fucked up because of what you experienced as a kid. Just because your dad acted like a dick doesn't mean that your boyfriend will. It's really not fair to judge him by the way your dad behaved. If it is meant to be, it will be.*

CBT involves using behavioral strategies to interrupt negative thoughts.

- When I feel anxious about partner infidelity, I take five slow, deep breaths and repeat the word "calm" to center myself. I also try to take a walk to clear my mind.

CBT encourages using positive affirmations or coaching statements to counter the negative and give us focus and improve our mood.

- For example, I tell myself I am choosing to be different from my mother. *I will not live in that prison, waiting for my partner to cheat. It's not real.*

Here are some other examples of CBT and how it works:

- **Prove the thought is true, or ask yourself if it is helpful.**
  Thought: People don't like me.
  Proof: I have a lot of friends. I am a pretty nice person. I help out at work. I seem to be well liked by people I meet. Really, there is no evidence. This is just how I feel about myself sometimes. I can't prove it. It also isn't a very nice or helpful thing to say to myself.

- Argue with negative thoughts by finding new ways to look at the situation.

  Thought: Bad things happen to me.

  Argument: I tend to see bad things because I am looking for them. I am going to write down one positive thing every morning and every afternoon to remind myself to see both sides.

- Use thought stopping, distraction, or affirmations

  Thought: I'm not good enough.

  Thought Stopping: Say *Stop* or *No!* Write *I am not going there today*.

  Distraction: Go do something else like exercise.

  Affirmations: Tell yourself *You are worthy. You can do whatever you set your mind to. You are strong. You are a survivor.*

MINDFULNESS

Another very effective technique for managing dysfunctional core beliefs and negative self-talk is mindfulness. Because mindfulness is all the rage right now, you've probably heard of it.

It's really quite simple. Mindfulness is forcing yourself to be aware of what is going on at that moment—and wow, is it ever hard to do consistently. It may be easy to do for one moment, but then you probably notice your mind jumping all over the place. The trick to mindfulness is sticking with the moment and not giving up.

So, perhaps in the moment, I notice I am feeling anxious. I identify it and sit with it. I become observant. Maybe I become aware of all kinds of negative self-talk. Maybe I become aware of a lot of triggers around me. I just notice it all. Think of it as heightened awareness without reactivity.

Mindfulness is very different from CBT. Mindfulness is intentionally trying to be in the present, noting the negative thoughts about the past and future, and letting them go. Mindfulness does not advocate arguing with your thoughts. It is just being aware of them and not reacting.

With mindfulness, you recognize what is happening and what you are thinking and respond with: *Oh, there I go again with the story of how I am not good enough or how I have to please others. I am going to stop judging myself. I will let the thoughts be. They will pass.*

A mindfulness view of painful thoughts and emotions is that they are like cramps: You feel them. You identify that they hurt but aren't dangerous. They don't mean you need to go to the ER. You know they will pass. On the other hand, maybe the pain is chest pain, and you do need to go to the ER. Mindfulness is naming and understanding and deciding what to do.

With mindfulness, we accept that things may not be the way we want, but they are what they are. That battle is in the past, and it is over. Replaying it repeatedly does not change anything, and it isn't helpful anymore. The problem happens when we get into judging situations and ourselves as *bad*: that causes distress. The gap between where we find ourselves and where we want to be is the source of the pain. Mindfulness is about accepting where we find ourselves, instead of judging it and fighting it.

To be clear, this is not the same thing as saying we give up and accept defeat. It is about saying things are how they are—and *now* what do I want to do with that?

Mindfulness, like CBT, is helpful for many people, although it is a little harder to apply because it involves acceptance. Again, acceptance does not mean you call it good: acceptance is about acknowledging reality for what it is.

All the bitching and moaning and self-pity doesn't change anything. It just makes us feel worse, all while we are still in that bad spot—kind of like putting salt on a wound. The thing is that acceptance is not judging or denying: it is getting yourself away from rigid ideas of right and wrong, good and bad. The practice of being at peace with one's thoughts and letting go takes a lot of discipline and even more practice.

Mindfulness is consciously paying attention to the moment as it is happening. It is being aware of what is going on, what we are thinking, and how we are feeling. It is an intense observation without judging or critiquing—because when you get caught up in negative emotions, you cannot accurately see what is happening: you become distracted. Mindfulness is noticing. It is all part of intentional self-awareness. You are aware so you can intentionally decide how to best use the information.

Mindfulness is teaching ourselves to stop reacting to what is going on around us. Instead, we observe events and how we feel. Then we can develop a thoughtful response that is not impulsive. Mindfulness doesn't concern itself with the *content* of negative thoughts we have or the validity of those thoughts. Rather, it is the practice of being in each moment while it is happening without judging the moment or what is going on. Pain is viewed as a necessary part of life. Instead of trying to run from pain, we try to understand it through reflection, not rumination.

It is useful to reflect on the past and ask what can be learned. Reflection is thoughtfully considering what is happening, without all the emotional judgments. Rumination is obsessive, negative reviewing of the past over and over again and results in getting stuck in the emotional quicksand. Reflection is seeing a pitfall, noting a pitfall, and using that data to navigate henceforth.

Rumination is like pouring accelerant on a dumpster fire. This is what it looks like: *I was a terrible lover. I let myself go. I should have been more adventurous. I shouldn't have complained so much. That is why she left me. I sucked. I still suck. I will always suck. I am never going to find anyone.* Over and over. And so on.

Reflection is noticing and observing your thoughts and reactions without jumping into believing them or critiquing them.

Reflection is about wonder. This is reflection: *I didn't feel like having sex every night. I should have talked about how I felt instead of brushing her off again. Oh, there I go "shoulding" myself again. Wow. I do that a lot. Is there something I need to change about how I communicate, or is it just me judging again?*

Here are the fundamentals of mindfulness:

- Be aware of how you are feeling while you are feeling it. Be aware of what you are thinking while you are thinking it. You do this by purposefully practicing paying attention. Meditation is one way to practice this, but it is not the only way. There is a lot out there on meditation—whole books, even. I am going to focus on alternative mindfulness strategies.

Let's consider my previous example from the section on CBT (the one where I worry about my partner cheating on me). Here are some mindfulness strategies:

- I keep a journal; and when I feel the familiar fear of my partner cheating and fear of being alone and rejected, I write down my thoughts and feelings. I don't argue them: I just notice what is going on and name it. I name the feelings. I name the thoughts. I name the beliefs. I connect them together. I don't judge them or tell myself not to think or feel. The more I do this, the better I get at noticing until I don't have to write them down anymore. After I notice, I take three deep breaths and notice how the feelings change. I remind myself that my thoughts and feelings are part of the life story my family created for me. I accept that, but I also choose to not continue writing that same story. I am not buying into it today. I journal at the end of the day, putting all my observations in a cohesive story. I visualize myself letting my thoughts go like helium balloons.
- I imagine my thoughts are cars that are passing by. I notice how they race through my mind. I let them come and go.

- I notice the painful story of my past, and I visualize its being separate from me as a core person. I visualize it as a chapter in my book, but I am turning the page. I remind myself that I am not there *now*.
- I focus purposeful attention on what I am doing for a few minutes each day and just be there, in that place, while I am there. I notice right here right now.
- I stop looking at my smartphone, computer, and television while I eat meals. I try to appreciate how food tastes while I chew and take my time while eating. I start doing one thing at a time and stop multitasking. I set up technology-free times for myself.
- I ask myself if I need to do anything, or if my thoughts and reactions are self-created pain.

Self-created pain is the worst. With the example I've been using, perhaps I focus on how helpless I feel. I make the situation worse. When I make the situation worse by rumination, self-pity, and telling myself horrible stories about how bad things are, that is self-created pain, which is also called the second arrow.

THE SECOND ARROW

Consider this Buddhist story. You are walking the woods. It's a beautiful day. You are enjoying fresh air and relaxation. Suddenly, you are struck by an arrow that passes right through your body. It hurts like hell. You are completely freaked out. WTF?!

The fact that an arrow struck you is a fact. You can't change it. You can't control it. That part is done. What comes next is, however, under your control. When you start bitching and moaning: "Why did this happen? OMG, what if I lose my arm? What if I get an infection? Who will pay my bills? Who did this to me?!", you create your own suffering by self-inflicting a *second* arrow. I am going to ask you to call yourself out when you are creating or increasing your personal suffering by ruminating, lamenting, or generally feeling sorry for yourself. It is a complete waste of time, and you need to move on.

If our pain is self-created, we sit with it. Let it be. We notice our minds judging, and call it for what it is. We remind ourselves that sometimes events bring up baggage from the past. We don't have to carry the baggage. Remember, just the fact that we have a negative feeling doesn't mean we have done something wrong. Perhaps the negative feeling is about a storyline from the past that is starting to play in our minds telling us we need to please, must try to fix, or need to feel worthy.

Ideally, I would learn to listen to how I felt at the time, and it would become easier to identify what emotional baggage was being triggered. This new awareness would allow me to just note what was happening and not respond. I would learn to say to myself:

- Let it go.
- Let it be.
- Things are as they are.
- It is what it is.
- It is just the way it is supposed to be.

Mindfulness is a powerful tool, but it is one that takes great effort, time, and practice. If you combine mindfulness and CBT, the results are even better. You can pick and choose what strategy works best for you in each circumstance. The key is figuring out what works for you and when it works the best.

But wait: there's more!

POSITIVE PSYCHOLOGY

Although positive psychology has been around since the existential humanism developments of the mid-1900s, the formal positive psychology movement began in the late 1990s.[2] Positive psychology is the study and application of factors related to happiness, contentment, satisfaction, optimism, hope, meaning, and other positive emotional states. So much of psychology has focused— and continues to focus—upon what is wrong with people. It is easy to lose sight of all the uplifting things about people and the environment that lead to well-being. We sometimes forget to focus on what is strong and right and working well. This is the emphasis of positive psychology,[2] and it is the basis for this book. Too often, we focus on the negative. As I said, it is how our brains are wired, but it isn't everything.

Positive psychology sometimes gets a bad rap because it is mischaracterized as *don't worry, be happy.* Positive psychology is not simply telling oneself to think happy thoughts and forget negative thoughts. It is not pretending to be happy when we are not happy. It is not ignoring things in our lives that might cause unhappiness. If a person just ignores things that cause unhappiness, nothing ever gets fixed. Rather, positive psychology is the scientific examination of what makes people happy and well. It is the study of techniques that improve mood. Although there are things that are genetic and fixed, positive psychology examines how this can be taught and altered.

Currently, there is a tremendous amount of research being done on the many, many different applications of positive psychology on psychological and physical health. Some popular examples of positive psychology techniques include:

- keeping a gratitude journal where you write regularly about things you are grateful for

- writing thank-you notes to those who have impacted your life
- creating positive visualizations and practicing positive affirmations that are encouraging
- practicing random acts of kindness

The point of these activities is to consciously focus on positive emotions. It is too easy to skip right by the good things and focus on the negative. Positive psychology is becoming intentional about increasing positive feelings in your life.

Positive psychology techniques may overlap with CBT and mindfulness. For example, there may be times when we notice negative thoughts and try to replace them with affirmations or positive thoughts or argue back with positive self-talk. There may be times when we distract ourselves by being around people who are uplifting, or we may notice we are spending too much time around people who are negative, which is contagious. Positive psychology is more a philosophy that can be mixed with other therapeutic approaches.

But wait: there is even more. Here is where shit gets, shall we say, real.

THE PROFANE TWIST

I have had success in using CBT, mindfulness, and positive psychology. One day, I got the bright idea of also using humor and profanity as positive psychology techniques, even though I hadn't seen any studies saying, *"add #%$&!@ to your practice."*

Because my core beliefs revolve around following the rules, I thought I might get ex-communicated from my profession for suggesting swearing and humor in the therapy room. I decided to look at the scientific literature for support. Admittedly, there wasn't a shit ton; but to my surprise, this did prove to be a valid domain of scientific study.

My self-talk here was *Wow, you aren't entirely crazy.*

PROFANITY AND PSYCHOLOGY

I will assume that if you are reading this book, I won't have to work very hard to convince you that using profanity can help you feel better and function better. Just for fun, however, let me make a case that there *is* science between the use of swearing and well-being.

I am confident that you were told as a child (like I was) that swearing is inappropriate. It is considered vulgar, rude, rebellious, irreverent, offensive, and even evil by some. It is not something we want children to do.

I was not allowed to swear as a child; but, in retrospect, there is little wonder that I grew up to swear. It is generally not considered effective parenting to tell your children not to do something that you do yourself. Both of my parents swore in front of me, although I think my parents would say they used "conventional" cursing (damn, shit, hell). *Fuck* was never something I heard at home. I learned that word at school. I guess my parents had *some* standards.

As children, we learn that cussing is disrespectful, hooligan behavior, and off-limits. So *of course* we want to do it. Swearing is a behavior we reserve for adults, because adults are supposed to have the wisdom to be able to decide where and when to use profanity. Adults are supposed to have the ability to not speak all possible thoughts, and to use discretion about the utility of curse words.

The taboo nature of profanity is exactly why it is so effective. If we learned to cuss as an everyday part of language, then it wouldn't be so powerful. We save it to really emphasize a point or get some attention.

At Harvard, they study profanity, which means really smart people think cussing is legitimately valuable. According to Steven Pinker, Ph.D.,[3] a neurolinguist, there are multiple functions of swearing. Profanity can be:

- **Abusive:** meant to intimidate or offend another person
- **Cathartic:** meant to release pent-up emotion
- **Dysphemistic:** meant to communicate a negative impression of a subject
- **Emphatic:** meant to emphasize a point
- **Idiomatic:** meant to do nothing in particular; just an everyday vocabulary word

Swearing may also increase our sense of control in a bad situation. It can help us feel less like a victim and more empowered.[4] Swearing has positive psychological effects!

Benjamin Bergen, Ph.D.,[5] wrote a whole book on the scientific study of profanity. Apparently, science shows that cussing also provides health benefits, specifically increased pain tolerance, according to multiple studies. I shit you not.

Here is the scenario: Take two groups of people, and expose both to painful stimuli. One group is told to use a cuss word when they feel pain, and the other is told to use a neutral word. The group that is told to cuss is able to tolerate the pain significantly longer and reports feeling a lower level of pain overall.

The theory is that the brain processes swear words differently from everyday words. The automatic physiological reaction (or shall I say the release of emotions) associated with cussing allows people to tolerate more pain.

Let me push the envelope even further. There is evidence that people who curse for emphasis are judged to be more genuine.[6] When participants were asked to read stories or share opinions, the ones who were asked to swear in their account were perceived by others as being more believable and more persuasive.

A real-life example of this was present in a recent gubernatorial election in Michigan. One of the candidates drove home her point by emphasizing public sentiment about the poor conditions of roads. In her commercials, she repeatedly said we need to fix the "damn roads." She won, in part, because she captured the shared public sentiment of frustration associated with infrastructure inertia. She was viewed as genuinely charged up to do something.

Cursing in these circumstances is a sign of sincere passion in order to persuade an audience who might otherwise question authenticity.

Who knew swearing had legitimate functions other than rebellion against proper etiquette?

I don't believe that using profanity willy-nilly somehow improves mood: it is the intentional use of profanity with humor aimed to alleviate emotional pain. Let me again emphasize the word "intentional." What I am suggesting is that we combine laboratory research and design clinical interventions with the goal of changing negative thoughts and feelings.

Based on his investigations, Timothy Jay, PhD.,[6] believes swearing leads to a cathartic effect and that using profanity combined with humor leads people to report feeling relief. In fact, Dr. Jay suggests that swearing may actually lead to diminished aggression, because people who use targeted profanity will have released the anger, leaving them less likely to act on it.

When I think of cussing, I think of laughing, probably because it is some of that inappropriate rebellion in me.

HUMOR AND PROFANITY

I have long heard that humor and laughter are antidotes to negative emotions. I consider this to be positive psychology. Humor has been shown to be effective in relieving depression, anxiety, and sleep disturbances. It is thought to relieve tension under stressful circumstances because it can make reality less threatening. It is cathartic.[6] It is a positive coping technique and survival skill in a crazy world.[6]

According to incongruity theory, when we see things that violate our expectations or find something threatening (e.g., we realize the shit has hit the fan), we may laugh to make the threat more manageable.[7] There is also evidence to support this idea. Zhao, Zhang, Li, Wang & Chen[8] add that humor is even more effective when it is considered to be *inappropriate*.

What is more inappropriate than using profanity and humor to talk back to yourself?

Burton[4] believes swearing is funny. Profanity imparts perspective to a situation, and adds lightheartedness while pushing social norms at the same time.[4] In addition, swearing and humor help create a sense of belonging with others, a feeling of being honest about how we feel, and a fun-loving attitude. When we use humor to poke fun at ourselves, it can improve our connections with others and increase our comfort with making mistakes.[9]

The bottom line is: swearing is a form of self-expression, a positive stress-coping tool, *and* a way to connect to others around us.

SUMMARY

This chapter was all about helping you understand some of the best tools we have in psychology for feeling better. CBT has been around for a long time, is well studied, and works. Mindfulness and positive psychology are more recently receiving a lot of attention. They make a lot of intuitive sense and are easily compatible with CBT. Humor and profanity are not as mainstream—yet. All these tools are fantastic, but what if they could be combined in a more unified way? What if they could be made intuitively useful and *fun*? That is where MOMF comes in. Now things get super-interesting.

2

MOMF

M ove on, Motherfucker, or MOMF, is my saucy twist to the ideas presented in chapter one. Now that you know there is a bona fide science that supports a psychological benefit to the targeted use of profanity, you will see that this is a legit strategy. I am not talking about helter-skelter profane diatribes: I am talking strategy here. It's evidence-based.

I will assume that if you are reading this book, swearing doesn't offend you. I have written extensively (e.g., *Move on Motherf*cker: Live, Laugh & Let Sh*t Go*[10]) about the legitimate use of profanity for psychological health. It is also a technique I use in my private practice and personal life. I call it MOMF, pronounced "mom-f."

I use MOMF with a lot of people, but I find that people are exceptionally receptive to MOMF after a breakup. I think it is because they are already engaging in military-grade profanity by the time we meet, and so it seems a natural evolution.

After a breakup, there is so much pain, and it is oozing everywhere. During times like these, we search for that next level of language that captures the essence of our anguish. Although we find that little erases the pain, cursing is better than setting the house on fire. It is, in fact, a valid method of releasing pain.

To be clear, MOMF is not simply adding profanity to preexisting evidence-based techniques. No, MOMF is an ideology with intentionality. The premise is that we are each accountable for the role we play in our own suffering. The implication is that we play the motherfucker role by choice. It is acknowledgement that we can stop or change at any time we like. It is the intentional use of profanity as a way of holding ourselves accountable when we play victim to circumstance.

If you already feel victimized by someone in a relationship, why the hell would you want to victimize yourself further? MOMF is about recognizing what you are doing and calling yourself out.

And please don't be offended when I refer to you as *motherfucker*. I mean it in a good way—like a friend. I'm telling you to move on and get over yourself because you are the one holding yourself back: i.e. you are being a *motherfucker*. How do I know this? Because you are human, and that is what we humans do. We aren't rational. We beat ourselves up. We judge. We overthink, and we care *way* too much about what others think. In other words, we get in our own way. So, it's time to *move on, motherfucker*.

MOMF is self-love. By calling yourself out, holding yourself accountable, laughing with yourself, and accepting your own humanity, you are more likely to heal. This is self-compassion.

You have the power. You are the motherfucker in charge. Your automatic thoughts don't dictate your destiny, and you don't even have to argue with them. You can just laughingly say to yourself "Shut. The. Fuck. Up. I'm not listening to you, crazy motherfucker."

As Elizabeth Lesser[11] suggests, we are all just "bozos on the bus." We have to stop thinking we are the only ones with shit-show lives. It feels too lonely there, and the truth is that there is no other bus for the people who have their shit together. Telling ourselves that there is a better bus is cruel. There is only one kind of bus, and all of us are on it together—*with* our unique shitshows.

These are empowering thoughts, because they reinforce autonomy, control, and choice.

WTF?

So, while your parents may have taught you that cursing makes you look like a punk, the scientific community would argue that profanity has a valid function in communication. Indeed, cussing may even indicate to others that you are genuine and believable. There is a time and place for everything. It is the judicious use of profanity that makes it so effective.

Emma Byrne,[12] author of *Swearing Is Good For You*, argues that profanity should not become commonplace in language because if it does, it loses its punch. Byrne suggests that when swearing is used in a skillful manner, it is "socially and emotionally essential."

When I read all this, I thought *Fuck, yeah! I knew it!*

All of that said, I didn't know of anyone who was using this information in counseling with patients. I didn't learn about this in school. I hadn't read about it in journals. I hadn't heard about it from colleagues. It wasn't being taught at the latest conferences. All I knew was that profanity, humor, CBT, positive psychology, and mindfulness worked for me and my patients, particularly for folks recovering from a breakup. There is so much pent-up emotion and pain. The mind is consumed with negative thoughts and searingly painful feelings.

In this book, I specifically apply the principles of MOMF to breakups. I take CBT, mindfulness, positive psychology, and, yes, profanity and humor to help people get a grip—to better understand what happened, how it happened, and where to go next so things get better. It is a complicated process.

Interested? Read on.

THE SKINNY ON MOMF

MOMF is a mash up of CBT, mindfulness, positive psychology, humor, and profanity that creates an enhanced level of catharsis aimed to reduce the psychological pain that interferes with growth.

First, you identify your core negative belief, your genetic predispositions, and your negative self-talk patterns. This is CBT. You become an expert on catching the negative thoughts, and you label that self-talk as the inner motherfucker. When you notice that you are listening to the negative, critical, judgmental, and painful self-talk, you call yourself out as being the motherfucker in the scenario, behaving in ways that aren't healthy. Deciding to move on from that is MOMF'ing. The term "motherfucker" allows you to laugh at the ways you play a part in your own problems. This is the humor and positive psychology part. It allows you to acknowledge your own part in the problem and hold yourself accountable for making improvements. Mindfulness is actively seeking to let go and end the abuse of the second arrow.

MOMF is being intentional and accepting that you are actively causing and perpetuating your own pain. And you can stop doing this any time you are ready to work at it. This intentionality is a key part of being successful. It is about feeling empowered in your role to change. It is about hope. It is about being effective.

Let me say again: calling yourself a motherfucker is not at all meant to be derogatory. It is not meant to be abusive. I see the term *motherfucker* as interchangeable with *friend*. It is harnessing the ability to talk to yourself like a confidant and call out the bullshit of self-defeating choices by saying "enough, already."

TINO'S MASHUP:

Tino was on his second major relationship breakup in a year. He was thirty years old, and he felt time was running out on his future. He wanted to get married and have a gaggle of kids. Work was going well, but he felt like his personal life sucked balls. Tino turned to binge-drinking for a few days, but that wasn't helping him feel better. His friends suggested a strip club, but he'd been down that lonely path too: it never ended well.

He had a core belief that guys should be in committed relationships by the time they were twenty-six. He started telling himself he was clearly not a great catch, or he'd be like all his friends: getting married. He had this negative self-talk: *I'm a loser. No one wants me.*

Tino decided to MOMF. He did this:

- He reminded himself that just because he had thoughts of being a loser didn't make the thoughts true. He told himself another breakup was a real disappointment, but it was done. Over. In the past. And the feelings of sadness were natural. At this point, all he could control was how long he was going to stab himself with the second arrow.
- Tino called out the role he was playing as the motherfucker. He was feeling sorry for himself and punishing himself, which only added to the genuine disappointment.
- He wrote down counterstatements and affirmations. He forced himself to get out of bed and exercise. Tino admitted to himself that his previous relationship had been one of convenience. He wasn't really all that into his girlfriend, but he'd hoped she

would change as he helped her grow as a person. He allowed himself to sit with the disappointment and feel the pain. He observed what he would like to change, based on the reality of his situation.

- Tino accepted himself for who he was at that moment, not who he feared or fantasized about. He was honest about the things he could learn (e.g., that he should never settle for less than he wanted and that he can't change others) and improve about himself, and he made a plan to move on.

- He began a gratitude journal. Every day, he wrote something he was grateful for, and he set a goal of doing one good deed for someone else.

- Tino developed salty language to argue back with his negative self-talk. He had a good laugh at the level of his self-pity. Tino thought of what his best friend would say to him: "Fucker, you've got to work for what you want. It takes time and effort. Don't you dare settle for less. Get off your ass and live your life!" This would make Tino smile. He tried to poke fun at himself and see the humor when he visualized himself throwing a temper tantrum. This made him laugh aloud as he thought of crazy things in his past that had made him behave in crazy ways. Tino argued back with his negative self-talk: *Shit didn't go as planned, but you are not helpless. Fuck that.*

- Tino used MOMF lingo to let go of the pain he was hanging on to. He said, "This sucks, but this was obviously meant to happen. What does it mean for me? Stop making it worse. Get off your ass, you sexy thing."

- He detached from pain with these thoughts: *It is what it is, fucker, whether you like it or not. Life is going forward, and you are not giving up.* He moved on to think: *Clearly, that shitshow wasn't meant for me. I guess I dodged a bullet in reality. There is something even better out there for me, but I won't find it on my couch. I need to get my ass in gear so I'll be ready. What do I need to do differently?*

- He used positive psychology to encourage himself. He used an online meme generator. He created some funny Samuel L. Jackson memes using profanity and positive coaching statements to encourage himself when he felt down. He posted these around his house.

- Tino also decided to make a gratitude jar where he forced himself to think of one thing each day he was grateful for.

- He forced himself to get up and move. He called a friend.

- He sat with his worst-case scenario: that he would stay single. He asked himself if he could realistically deal with that outcome. The longer he sat with it, the more manageable it felt. Tino decided he was going to research getting a rescue animal to help himself feel less lonely. (Sitting with his worst-case scenario causes Tino to habituate to his scary thoughts and images by forcing him to sit with them. The fear gets old and wears off—as long as he is not adding to the scenario and embellishing.) Once Tino habituates, he can MOMF. Plus, the worst possible outcome probably won't happen anyway. He will be prepped if it does, and relieved when it doesn't.

- He asked himself: *If I knew I would die today, would I spend one more minute thinking about this shit?* If the answer was yes, it meant he had unfinished business to take care of, like apologizing or asking for forgiveness. If the answer was no, then he needed to move on, motherfucker, because at this point he was just torturing himself—being self-abusive—which is of no benefit to anyone. Much of what we worry about is a complete waste of time. Putting it in this context generally helps that become more clear.

MOMF'ing is understanding there are certain dysfunctional patterns of thinking we can't eradicate because they have been emotionally learned earlier in life, like pleasing others or feeling not good enough. In other words, we've been mindfucked in our history. We can acknowledge those patterns and see them in ourselves (mindfulness). When the negative self-talk that stems from dysfunctional patterns of thinking pops up, we can say *There is the brainwashing (mindfulness). Move on, motherfucker, because you know where it will lead if you listen (MOMF). You'll go to crazy town again. Crazy town is uncomfortable, and then you say and do things you wish you hadn't (CBT). Learn from the past (mindfulness). Move on, motherfucker. Don't do this to yourself.* Adding in positive psychology with gratitude and affirmations is a bonus.

If you want to know more about how to use MOMF techniques with a variety of issues, read *Move on Motherf*cker: Live, Laugh & Let Sh*t Go*. It will give you more practice on how the techniques apply to many areas of life.

This book is about you and your breakup. Move on, motherfucker.

· GETTING THERE ·

At this point, I highly recommend starting a journal. It will help you identify themes in your core beliefs, self-talk, relationships, and life. It will help you organize your thoughts and self-reflect. It will help you track your progress over time. Journaling is a highly effective tool, and I will suggest a lot of writing exercises. Don't worry, no one cares about grammar or penmanship. This is all for you, baby.

Get out your journal now. After reading this intro, ask yourself what dysfunctional beliefs you can identify about yourself, other people, and the world. What kind of negative self-talk do your core beliefs generate? How do these affect your relationships? How have they colored your perceptions about relationships? It's early in the process, but what is beginning to look like it needs to change? Write about these in your journal. See what feelings bubble up. Take a deep dive and see where it goes.

People often ask me how to journal. There is no one way. You just write thoughts and feelings that come to mind. When you worry too much about *how*, you are deep into judgment territory. There is no right or wrong. It just about self-exploration. Go where you need to go. Notice, and then decide what you might want to do with the new insight.

RECOMMENDED READING

Burns, David, M.D. *The Feeling Good Handbook*. New York: Plume, 1999.

Harris, Russ, M.D. *The Happiness Trap*. Boston: Trumpeter, 2008.

Eckleberry-Hunt, Jodie, Ph.D. *Move on Motherf*cker: Live, Laugh & Let Sh*t Go*. Oakland: New Harbinger, 2020.

3

You Will Survive

There is much I need to tell you, but first things first. Right after a breakup, I understand that you are just working to get through the day. The survival part is the worst.

JANELLE'S STORY

Janelle looked like a natural-disaster survivor. Her hair was disheveled. She wore yoga pants and an oversized sweatshirt, which was fine, but they looked like they had been worn for a week with food stains on them. Her face was puffy. Her eyes were swollen, and she had a constant stream of tears down her face. In fact, she had a hard time talking because she would seize up with deep, silent sobs of pain and sadness.

Janelle's partner of five years had left her two nights ago for someone else. She had no fucking clue. Yeah, she knew things had gotten a little stale in the relationship, but she hadn't known it was *that* bad. Janelle's partner refused to speak to her at all. She said it felt like her heart had been ripped out of her body. She wasn't eating. She wasn't going to work. She wasn't doing any-thing other than crying.

Janelle could only participate in bits and pieces of discussions because her mind kept wandering. She said hours would pass and she had no idea what had been going on. Relief would come if she could sleep, but it was still fitful. Then, she would wake up with that sick ache that the nightmare was real.

In chapter 4, I give more detail and hope for what comes after survival—because this time will pass, but none of that matters right now because you feel like you can't breathe. You have a nasty feeling in your body. You cannot imagine how you are going to go on from here. You hurt to the bone. That is what a breakup feels like when it is with someone you love. It is hard to even think clearly. So let's first focus on life support in this moment.

This chapter is about survival.

THE BASICS

First off, congratulations for picking up this book—not that it will change your life or anything, but you are doing something. That is what counts. You are showing up for the fight. Take one day at a time. Even if you are only able to read a couple of pages a day, that's okay. This chapter is about doing what you can, and every step helps.

I don't mean to sound too parental, but at times like this people may need a reminder of how to walk—one foot in front of the other. If this chapter seems too elementary for you, skip it. It is definitely more focused on the immediate aftermath of a breakup.

What I tell people who come into my office right after a breakup is "You will feel better. You will. I can't say exactly when, but it *will* happen."

I know you are wondering what is next.

This is not a hard-and-fast rule, but generally I think the first two weeks post-breakup are the worst. After that, it is still hard, but it gradually gets better. After a month, you will be sore but healing. After three months, you will be feeling closer to your baseline.

I don't say this because I can predict the future, and it may not apply exactly to you. It is just what I have learned from working with folks post-breakup. Having some sort of guideline can be the thread that holds it all together. It gives you some kind of expectation of when the pain will lessen. It is hope.

This rough timeline is true *only if* you have stopped contact with your ex. There are times people come to me and say "I broke up with my girlfriend, but we still talk and text." Okay, this is not what "broke up" looks like. The clock starts on healing when the entire relationship is over, when the contact ends. Think of every unnecessary contact as breaking open the wound again. Every time a wound breaks open, healing has to start over.

I sometimes wish the world were as black-and-white as I just made it sound. It isn't. There are times when two people live together or are married and have to communicate around division of property. There are times when children are involved, and custody and visitation are involved. There are times when life will just not allow a cease and desist around communication.

If communication can end, great. Let it. If not, ask yourself how you can set limits on it. You may have to communicate about child visitation, but you don't have to get updates on your ex's social life or daily troubles. Seemingly helpful check-ins to see how you are doing aren't helpful. They fuck with your mind. You start to wonder if the person still cares. You analyze why the person is thinking about you. You stop and tell yourself how thoughtful the person is and how tragic it is that things are over. Then you wonder if maybe it really isn't over after all.

The point is: any communication brings that person and the past and the pain into the forefront of your mind. We need to stop this.

There are the times I hear about exes sending long, critical texts that are berating and meant to stir up trouble. My recommendation: *delete*. While there may be some things that need your attention, there are also many that don't. You no longer care about problems that don't affect you. You no longer care about opinions and criticisms. You are no longer beholden to listen to the bullshit, and you don't need to just say "hi" when it hurts to do so.

Set boundaries where you can. Stick to those boundaries. Block the other person if they cannot respect your limits. It isn't meant to be rude: it is meant to self-protect. You may be surprised to admit to yourself that you need to communicate far less than you previously thought. Many kids have their own phones and can call you when needed without involving the other parent.

I readily admit I do not believe you can *just be friends* after a breakup either. Too much has happened. Too many feelings are involved. Plus, if you ever get into a romantic relationship with someone else, the other person will not be down with you being all friendly with your ex. Why would you want to bring that baggage with you into the future anyway?

And let's be even more honest: Is this what true friendship looks like? Doubtful.

I digress.

My point here is that the first order of business is to limit contact to only the absolutely necessary. And you can only control your own behavior.

Sometimes I hear that a person is enjoying a rare moment of

peace, and then the ex makes random contact, and it is experienced as traumatic. It is like being in the middle of a peaceful meditation, and acid rock music starts blaring out of nowhere. The unexpected contact stirs it all up again, even if it is meant to be helpful or harmless. It feels unpredictable, and it is triggering. Sometimes the intrusions are meant to keep things stirred up or continue toxic conversations. There is no need for this, particularly at this point when you are feeling so defenseless and hurt. Block the ex if at all possible. No emails. No texts. No phone calls. Sometimes this can even be helpful in shutting off your mind, which may be subconsciously waiting to hear something. If the ex is blocked, you can rest assured that there will be no contact.

SURVIVAL SKILLS

Now that you are in a spot of being truly broken up, here is my survival guide.

1. Make a daily schedule that is fairly basic. Set a time to be out of bed even if you don't have to be out of bed. Get your ass up even if you don't feel like it. Make yourself get dressed even if you don't have to get dressed. Put things on your schedule that will require you to leave the home. Make plans with friends. Take a walk. Go out to lunch. Make a run to the store. You are not allowed to say "I just don't feel like it" while crossing something else off the schedule.

2. Set a daily goal. If you're feeling ambitious, set more than one goal. Write it down. Post it on the fridge. At the end of the day, write down the shit you got done. That is progress. Make it a point to write down one or more things you

can celebrate: things that went well, things that you handled well. It may even be that you celebrate getting through most of the day without crying. It is a victory.

3. Note when your mind drifts to thoughts or images of your ex. Make a special effort to refocus your attention on something—anything that will distract you from those thoughts or images. Yell "Fucking asshole!" if it helps you. This is an actual CBT technique called thought-stopping. Don't you just love science?

4. Do not listen to sad songs. Do not watch sad movies. Do not look at photos of you and your ex on your dream vacation. Stay off social media. This is not the time. It's probably a good time to take photos of your ex off the wall or the desk so you're not seeing the image everywhere. No need to rub salt in the wound right now.

5. Do not drink alcohol or use mind-altering substances. This will make it more likely you will call, text, or stalk your ex, probably saying things you will regret. The day after will leave a double hangover—physical and emotional remorse. It's just not worth it.

6. Call or message your good friends and tell them what is going on. Don't replay it over and over with each one in gory detail, because that will not help. Tell them the essentials, that you need them now, and be specific about what you want from each one. Friends offer different things. Maybe one will make you laugh; another will be a good listener; and another will kick your ass. Set up your support system now. Put friends on your daily schedule that you are committed to following. No cancellations.

7. Schedule yourself to get some aerobic exercise for at least thirty minutes a day. Yoga can also be soothing, but be sure to get something aerobic as well. There is also something

healing about nature—getting fresh air and being surrounded by life. Get outside. Walk. Ride a bike. Move.

8. Use a calming visualization if you feel overwhelmed. I really
like visualizations by Belleruth Naparstek. They are very
soothing. Check out Belleruth's *Heartbreak, Abandonment &
Betrayal* on HealthJourneys.com. You may also find free
visualization on sites like YouTube to try, but I can personally recommend Belleruth's work as being healing.

9. Before bed, try a body scan by Jon Kabat-Zinn, free on
YouTube ("Jon Kabat Zinn Body Scan Meditation GUIDED
MEDITATION"). This is also something you can do at any
time when you need to soothe yourself. You may like it so
much that you will want to try meditation on a daily basis.
If so, Kabat-Zinn has a lot of content on YouTube, as well as
a shit ton of books. He is the best. There are also apps like
Calm and HeadSpace: Meditation and Sleep, which are popular meditation platforms. If you haven't already figured it out,
meditation is a great way to focus your brain.

10. When you feel flooded with emotion, take five very slow, deep
breaths. Breathe in so deeply that your belly protrudes. Hold
each breath for five seconds and then exhale very slowly. As
you do this, tell yourself "I'm okay. It's okay. This will pass."

11. Do something kind for yourself every day. Maybe you get a
favorite coffee, have a favorite dish, paint your toenails, light
a great-smelling candle, or treat yourself to a movie. Do this
for two weeks—just a daily sign of self-compassion. You can
wait for other people to do it for you, or you can give yourself
what you actually need in the here-and-now.

12. Go to Pinterest or another favorite site and find a new affirmation for each day—something that speaks to you, something
motivational or inspirational. Tape it on your refrigerator.
Write it on a journal page, and write a reflection about the
quote. Keep it in mind as your day unfolds. Remind yourself

of the affirmation—as kind of a lane-keep assist—to help you stay focused.

13. Get the book *The Reality Slap* by Russ Harris, M.D. Read a page or two every day. It is a book about accepting and experiencing the ups and downs of life and finding peace. It is emotionally soothing.

14. Catch your negative self-talk. Write it down. Argue back with it. Curse back at your inner bully. Tell your internal judge to *shut the fuck up*. Be kind to yourself. Give your inner victim a hand and pull him up. Dust them off. Empower them. Break the second arrow in half before someone gets hurt.

THAT FEELING OF PANIC

It is common to experience times when you feel like you're about to lose your shit. You may feel lightheaded or dizzy; your heart may race; you may feel like you can't breathe. This is what a panic attack feels like, and the most important thing I can tell you is that panic attacks typically pass in ten minutes or less. Remember that. They pass. This is important to tell yourself, because panic attacks are incredibly unpleasant. You actually feel like you may be losing your mind. Think of it as your brain saying *I'm on overload. I have to release some energy here*.

Our brains are wired for survival. In order to keep us alive, we have something called the fight-or-flight response. The fight-or-flight response is when the brain sends out signals to the rest of the body to get ready to fight off a threat or run like hell. Those signals raise our heart rate, blood pressure, and blood sugar, as well as many other physical responses, and this reaction occurs in response to anything we find threatening. Our brains don't always distinguish between the threat of someone trying to rob us and the threat of feeling alone.

Breakups are a prime time to experience panic. Because you are already so off-kilter, it can be even scarier to have a panic attack. Here are some suggestions for managing panic and panic attacks:

- Tell yourself it will pass.
- Do not try to fight it. The more you try to fight it, the worse it may feel.
- Take deep breaths very slowly through your nose, and breathe out through your mouth.
- Use grounding with your five senses: Describe what you see around you, what you hear around you, what you smell. Touch something. Ask yourself how it feels. Describe how different parts of your body feel.
- Do a guided visualization.

The best way to decrease panic attacks overall is to be sure you have regular aerobic exercise in your life. This will help decrease the tension-building in your body.

· GETTING THERE ·

Think about how you have managed past devastations—not just breakups. What worked to calm you down? What kinds of things generally work to soothe you now? Add your own ideas to the list of concrete things you can do to feel better.

We're starting slow here. We are not going from feeing completely destroyed to having a good time. Avoid the all-or-nothing thinking. Do the small things you identified until you begin to feel stronger. Think of this process as similar to recovering from the flu. You do what you can, not pushing it too hard but pushing a little, and each day you feel a bit stronger. One day you will find yourself feeling closer to the old you, and that is when the hard work of recovery really begins.

When you feel stronger, able to focus your attention, and are ready to get on with it, move on to chapter 4. Don't rush it. Listen to your body. It is wiser than you believe.

4

Somebody Please Give Me a Map

Now that you have some skills with which to settle yourself down, let's talk about what to expect going forward. Break-ups are losses—loss of a person in your life; loss of the life you expected; loss of a norm; loss of a friend; loss of a dream; loss of love. The pain of the loss is grief.

The grief process has some predictable markers. Knowing this can help you feel more normal and provide comfort because you are moving along in the healing, even if it doesn't always feel that way.

MIRABELLE AND VON

Mirabelle and Von were married for seven years. They were in love and had a great relationship for the first couple of years. They did things by the book and waited to have children until they'd bonded as a couple. Then, life happened kind of fast. They had three children in five years, and then things started to unravel. Von seemed to work all the time. When he was home, he was tired and just wanted to relax. Mirabelle was completely exhausted. She was desperate for Von to help more, so she nagged incessantly. Von began avoiding Mirabelle, and it became a negative cycle.

Mirabelle and Von went to marriage counseling, but all they did was argue. After things deteriorated further to where they were barely speaking, they decided to divorce. Mirabelle, in particular, was unhappy with this solution even though she agreed to it. She was angry and resentful of Von for running out on the family, but she also wanted to be "rid of him." At the same time, she was intensely sad about the end of their marriage. It was the end of her dream and the future she'd planned. The idea of starting over was revolting.

Mirabelle felt a little insane. Von told her she *was* crazy. She wondered if it was actually true.

They'd planned to raise the kids together. They'd dreamed about doing epic vacations. They'd wanted to move to an area where they could enjoy a lot of outdoor activities as a family. Mirabelle was sad things hadn't worked with Von, but she was even more melancholy that her life dreams were "ruined."

Despite everything, she believed he was a good guy deep down. He just couldn't get his shit together, and he could be a complete asshole. What had happened to the guy she'd met nine years ago?

Mirabelle didn't want to date. It was too hard. She didn't want another man playing dad with her kids. She couldn't even think about how things were going to work with splitting up everything with Von.

She hated how things were, but she was perplexed when she tried to consider how things would change. She felt hopelessly stuck, because there was no good outcome in her mind. She was on the roller coaster to nowhere, or at least that was how it felt. Mostly, she was experiencing heartbreak.

What Mirabelle had to learn was that all her thoughts, feelings, and experiences were normal. She just needed a way to sort them all out so they made some kind of sense to her.

THEORY OF GRIEF

Elisabeth Kübler-Ross[13] was a renowned psychiatrist, immortalized by her work in death studies. She wrote about the stages of grief in her classic 1969 book *On Death and Dying*.

The stages of grief are relevant to breakups. Think of a breakup as the death of a dream or idea. The feeling of loss is kind of the same. Not everyone goes through all of Kübler-Ross's stages, which I address in more detail below. Some don't go in order. Some follow the model perfectly.

Does it seem like I am talking out of both sides of my mouth? That's because the model is useful, but it isn't perfect.

Kübler-Ross's model gives practical information, but the bottom line is that we humans are messy and hard to capture with one theory. No one model is going to encapsulate all the marvelous parts of our unique shitshows.

What I like is that some of the ideas contained in end-of-life grief are helpful in understanding the emotional experience of breakups. It won't necessarily lay out a turn-by-turn road map of what will happen next, but it can really help alleviate the sense of losing one's mind. All of the roller-coaster conflicting emotions are normal. They are expected. And many people find comfort in the idea that there is a theoretical end. I say "theoretical" because I have seen people who never recover from a breakup. I mean that in the sense they don't want to recover: they *choose* not to. There are some people who want to hang on to the past. They want to ruminate and keep it front-and-center in order to keep the relationship alive. If a person wants to move on and grieve, there must be some willingness to let go. That isn't something I can give to you: it is something you can give to yourself.

The folks who don't move on seem to cling to the idea that if they remember the past, it somehow keeps their ex responsible. I can assure you the ex has moved on and doesn't give a shit. What keeping the past alive does do, however, is to eat at your soul.

Back to Kübler-Ross.

She proposed five stages of grief: **Denial, Anger, Bargaining, Depression,** and **Acceptance.** I took these stages and MOMF'd them up here, specifically for breakups. With each stage, I list some suggestions of things you can do to help you cope.

Keep in mind, again, that some people go through all of the stages. Some people hit some but not others. Some people go through them in a different order. The point of the description is to help you understand your emotional experience, not to tell you how to grieve.

Denial

(Excuse me, what the fuck just happened?)

In this stage, shock sets in. There can be feelings of numbness or horror. That sick aching that creeps over you, which you don't understand. There can also be terror about how things will go on . . . what will happen next. This leads to a strong desire to go on with life as usual—believing the relationship is not over, despite the knowledge that things were not going well.

The reality of the situation just isn't sinking in. It is as if none of it is real. There may even be moments where you believe it is not happening. There is absolutely a tendency toward false hope and a desire to hold on to the reality you want, rather than actual reality.

In all transparency, I hate this stage. People come to me

hoping I will tell them something they've missed—something that will fix it all and make it all go away. I realize I may come off as cruel and heartless because I am honest. I can only help people fix themselves. At this stage, folks aren't ready to hear truths or realities. They want to hear about miracles, misunderstandings, and fairy tales. They want to know how they can fix the other person.

I do not yet possess that kind of black magic.

Suggestions: Useful strategies for this stage were largely covered in chapter 2 under Survival Skills. Here, I will highlight some of those strategies again for review.

- Do not make contact with your ex, as hard as it may be. Any contact will not allow healing to begin. Journal the hell out of your feelings. (This will be super-important later, as you begin to see truths you'd missed earlier.)
- Surround yourself with supportive friends.
- Survive.
- Pay attention to when you are starting to tell yourself a Hallmark Channel story. Remind yourself of the facts. Things *are* how they seem.

Anger
(OMG! You are such a motherfucker!)

This is my favorite stage—because as anger sets in, people get a burst of energy. In this stage, there also may be distortions of reality—meaning you may not see things for what they are. Your anger may twist them into what fits your agenda. You may be plotting revenge.

One minute you may be up, and the next you are down. It can

feel like a war going on inside as part of you is mad as hell, and yet there may still be part of you that wants your ex back. You can entertain the idea that your ex wasn't perfectly amazing and wonderful, but you are still susceptible to missing the person you thought was great for you (or the fictional person you created in your mind).

Although you may recognize that your story wasn't a fairy tale, you may get pissed that it could have been if only _____ (your ex wasn't an asshole; you weren't such an asshole; space-time ceased to exist as we know it; and so on).

There may be a sense of *why me* or *this isn't fair*. Yes, there were good times, but there were very bad times too. There were red flags—things you missed or ignored. There was ugliness that you glossed over. You may even be mad at yourself for putting up with bullshit, but you can definitely point the finger at the role your ex played. Maybe you can see the role you played too.

Suggestions:

- Make a list of the red flags in your journal. Write about why you missed or ignored these. Write about how you will use this information in the future. Write about the things you did that contributed to things going wrong.
- Be kind to yourself. We all make mistakes. Learn. We are all human.
- Write about the things you need to let go and move on from. Let the revenge ideas go, by writing them down and ripping them up. Unfortunately, if you *don't* do this, they will only end up hurting you more (or landing you in jail!).
- Don't waste your time on the other person. Spend it on yourself. Get a punching bag or run your butt off. Discharge the anger in more productive ways.

Bargaining
(Please. Please take me back. I'll be good. I promise.)

This stage is when you beg and plead that you will change your ways if only you can get back what you has lost. Sometimes the begging and pleading is with the other person or with a higher power. If you were drinking too much or being too controlling, you promise to be different if given a second chance. You were blind, but now you see and are ready to fix what you weren't ready to fix before.

Suggestions:

- Practice mindfulness meditation. Focus on acceptance of the here-and-now. The thing is: you are who you are. You cannot and should not change to keep someone else. If it is meant to be, it will be.
- Perhaps this is an opportunity to learn and work on things to change, but it can't be to keep someone else. Someone leaving you also isn't about your being a good or a bad person: it is being sure that you are a good match for someone else. If you decide to make a change, do it for yourself.
- Get the right help. Consider professional counseling. This is the perfect time to get additional insight and tools to help you be the best version of yourself.

Depression
(Oh, shit. This hurts like hell!)

Hear me clearly state: this stage is not referring to depression as the clinical disorder. It is a stage that is unfortunately vernacularly named depression, and it refers to feeling sad and blue. Depression as a stage refers to normal and expected feelings. Depression as a disorder is an abnormal clinical condition. This stage, unresolved, absolutely can lead to depression as a disorder, but that isn't what I am addressing here.

In this stage, reality has set in, and there is overwhelming pain and then more pain and unending pain. You think and re-think. You analyze and play things over and over in your mind. You spend way too much time thinking about the *good ole days* when your partner was wonderful. You tell yourself you are doomed to be alone. You review—and review again—your faults, screw-ups, and negative qualities. You begin convincing yourself that happiness will be forever elusive.

In some respects, it's like revisiting some of the early devastation from chapter 3 on survival. As I mentioned, some of the characteristics of each stage bleed into one another.

People may be consumed with the emptiness, and again with the *why me* thoughts. Intense feelings of loneliness create an ache that goes straight to the bone. This stage can be incredibly hard, but I often find that people vacillate between this stage and anger, which provides some of those energy bursts.

I hate when people get stuck at this stage, because it is so heavy. Sometimes there is only negative thinking and feelings of hopelessness. At the same time, the pain of the depression stage is a necessary reality. Some people may see me as a sort of sadist, because I talk about embracing pain. It isn't so much that I feel like it is enjoyable that people experience pain, but that I understand there is a desire to skip past this, and often this is the stage where it is incredibly easy to jump into another relationship to ease the suffering. I know, however, that this is an eventual mistake. It only postpones the suffering for another day.

I look at pain through the lens of growth. In order to grow as humans, pain is essential. It is important that we allow it to happen so we can move on in a healthy way.

Suggestions: Again, these suggestions will be reminiscent of chapter 3.

- There is nothing I can give to make the pain go away, and that would not be helpful anyway. Stay away from alcohol or drugs, because they will make you say and do things you'll later regret. Resist the desire to numb your feelings.
- Don't listen to sad songs. Don't look at old photos. Don't watch sad movies. Make plans with good friends doing fun things. Go through the motions even if you don't feel like it.
- Keep busy.
- Be very good to yourself.
- Get out of bed. Get dressed.
- Set a goal. Eat healthy. Try yoga. Meditate.
- Keep writing the hell out of your feelings.
- Read *The Reality Slap* by Russ Harris.
- Remind yourself that it hurts when someone doesn't want to be with you or when things don't work out, but also remind yourself that you don't want to force anything. You want someone who can't wait to be with you. You want a relationship that builds you up. Never ever settle for less than you want—for less than you deserve.

Acceptance
(Good riddance, asshole!)

You now feel more comfortable in the relationship ending. It wasn't meant to be. You know—and feel—that that ending was right. You still feel pangs of sadness. You are not entirely over your anger, but you can laugh and joke. You are in the process of moving on. You think about jumping back into dating, but you know you need some time first to continue healing. You spend way less time thinking about your ex.

This stage is about accepting the new reality for what it is and deciding how to move forward. It can be scary, as one thinks about the future. Again, thoughts can become riddled with *What if I make the same mistakes again?* or *What if this happens again?*

Suggestions:
- Keep writing. Reflect on how you have grown, on what you have learned. Write your younger self a letter with particular focus on the red flags you missed. How will you prepare yourself not to do the same thing in the future?
- Make a list of qualities you must have in a future relationship. No compromises here. Set some goals for your future—independent of dating.

MOMF Stage
(I'm sorry, who?)

Kübler-Ross did not conceive of *move on, motherfucker*, but I feel like acceptance isn't the final end point. You can accept reality but still not be completely healed. For the MOMF stage, I think of transcendence—where you literally *have* moved on.

I see this stage as the point where you are so over it that you don't care about your ex. You don't get pissed. You don't get sad. You just don't care. You may even wish the person well or be glad you no longer have to deal with that bullshit. That is how you know you have completed the healing process.

I know it is super-hard, but the most important part is to be patient. The process takes time. There is nothing to speed it up (like jumping into a new relationship, which just creates new problems), and there is nothing to make it go away. You simply need to give it time and make healthy choices that will ease the pain.

Meanwhile, don't make it worse by telling yourself you will "never" be the same and will "never" feel better. Instead, treat it like a cold. *Great!* You feel like shit, but you know it will eventually pass. Sometimes it hangs on for longer, but it gradually improves, especially if we engage in self-care.

A lot of people don't make it here. They get stuck in anger or sadness, but that is carrying the toxicity from the past into the present. Those feelings only hurt you. Every life experience teaches us, if we let it. What a waste it would be to go through all the pain only to get stuck again and not learn the lesson presented to us. This stage is about that. It is about acknowledging that shit happened and it didn't work out, but you dealt with it. You reflected and learned, and you have moved on, motherfucker!

Suggestions:
- Live your life—the life you want. Leave the past in the past. Leave the future in the future. Be here in the now as you are, and be your best.

· GETTING THERE ·

Let me say this outright. Nothing will take away the pain of loss. There are no shortcuts to healing—and if there were, it would be like a guarantee that you would live it all again in the future.

It is incredibly important that you focus on taking care of yourself. Think about it like a friend. If you have a friend who is going through something awful and you can't fix it, you would do what you could for the friend to help. That is what self-care looks like. It is doing something for yourself like you would a friend. Self-care is ameliorating the pain by creating a cushion. It doesn't take the pain away.

I also want to say at the front end that you won't feel like doing any of this. That doesn't matter: you must do it anyway. In MOMF lingo, if you keep moving, you will eventually find yourself in a new environment. Go through the motions, and eventually your mind will catch up.

Here are some MOMF strategies you can use in all of the stages:

1. Go back to the dysfunctional core beliefs you identified in Chapter 2. How did these negative beliefs contribute to how you got to this point? What dysfunctional beliefs have driven your behavior up to this point? What do you want to do about it?

2. Now, write down your negative thoughts as you have them. How do they relate back to the core beliefs? Life hurts, but unwarranted self-criticism isn't helpful right now. If you are beating yourself up for refusing friends' calls and lying in bed eating ice cream, maybe you should do something about those behaviors. If you are beating yourself up for the past, it's a complete waste of time: you are only making yourself feel worse. Argue your asshole self-talk. Fight back like you mean it.

3. Call out the bullshit as you tell yourself yet another fairy tale about the *good ole days*. Well, they weren't so good in reality. In fact, they sucked. When you think about how romantic Carlie was on July 4th, you also have to remember how she got totally drunk and came on to several other friends before you had a huge fight at the end of the night. Sure, the next day was good as you both made up, but did any of this have to happen? Yes, there were good times, but be honest with yourself when you start to make your story into something it was not.

   Perhaps you say to yourself something like:

   "No more licking your own ass, my friend. Today, real life begins."

"Fake news!"

Maybe you write the fairy-tale story that you wanted and go back and edit it for facts. Write some MOMF commentary in the margins. When you wonder what to call out, think about what your best friend would say about your Disney version. "Oh yeah, but what about. . . ?"

4. Journal the shit out of your process. It will become abundantly clear how your distorted thoughts work, what patterns exist, and how you are growing. You will see progress over time. You will check yourself on bad days and celebrate the good. New insights will emerge. Be your own best friend.

5. Use MOMF'd-up affirmations. Get a new one every day. Use quotes that inspire and motivate you and keep you grounded on the path that you set out. Post them in your journal and around the house to keep yourself on the right path. Have some fun.

"Hello, hot stuff. And so, chapter two begins. . . ."

"Bitch, no more freebies to the questionable."

6. Be kind to yourself. Eat healthy. Go out with positive people. Keep busy. Force yourself to do fun things. Exercise, and exercise some more. Sweat out the toxicity. It will take a lot of effort, but it is worth it in the end. You will feel better, even if it feels exhausting to consider because, honey, you are so worth it. Take my word for it. You will never find someone who treats you well unless you believe you deserve it and demand it. Never, never settle for less than being happy. Life is just too damned short.

5

What's Love Got to Do with It?

In full disclosure, this chapter is a bit of bummer because I am going to take that fun and dreamy idea of love and douse it in cold, hard facts.

Unfortunately, this is going to contradict the Disney-themed fairy tales you've been told. In fact, that frog you've been kissing could very well give you warts.

While our hearts want to believe the fairy tales, our heads often know that doing so puts us at great risk. Our head wants us to focus on the facts.

In this chapter, I want to engage your head in understanding your heart.

Feelings are an incredibly important source of data, but it is important to recognize that feelings aren't always rational. In order to be successful at love, we have to recognize feelings and interpret them within the broader context of other facts and circumstances.

It is about using your head, and this chapter will help you do that. Yes, there is even a science in loving. The purpose of this chapter is to help you gain a solid understanding of love and what to expect in love, so you are in good shape to move on for good. Time to dive in.

THE EVOLUTION OF LOVE (BENNY AND LORENZO)

Benny and Lorenzo met when they were twenty-five. They started as friends in a larger group, but both quickly felt the connection. They started spending more time hanging out alone, and dating was a natural evolution of their relationship. Benny and Lorenzo shared many common interests and values. They just seemed to click easily.

Now they've been together for twenty years, and their relationship has changed a lot. Each of them has grown markedly as a human. The red-hot attraction they felt for one another twenty years ago has subsided. They are more comfortable disagreeing and arguing, knowing the other person won't just storm off and leave the relationship. There is a comfort with each being able to be themselves without fear of rejection. Benny and Lorenzo have survived many ups and downs in the relationship. They each describe an enduring love, respect, and friendship that feels much more like companionship.

Over the years, they each have wondered if the loss of the spark meant the end of the relationship. They wondered if it was a sign that they needed to move on. No one had ever told them what to expect, and popular culture had suggested that they should always be wildly into one another. They just didn't feel that way anymore. Was it normal? Was this a bad sign? Neither wanted to leave the comfort of their relationship, but was this just laziness? Were they lying to themselves?

The questions they have are common, but so few people have honest conversations about the answers.

I've seen one of two responses to the questions posed above.

One response is the *lipstick on the hog* posts on Facebook. What I mean by this is trying to make something ugly look pretty in spite of facts. They're fake. These are the ones that tell us if we aren't head over heels in love with our partner after twenty-five years, it is because we aren't trying hard enough. Barf.

The second response is the fear-based messages about how signs of boredom could be signs of an affair or risk of an affair. Better hire a private detective and start reading your partner's text messages. If you aren't having sex several times a week, something is clearly wrong.

Rarely do we hear the truth, which is that relationships get stale, and it does take work to keep it interesting. At the same time, no amount of work will keep it feeling like the first time. Only the band Foreigner can do that. (Google it.)

The problem for most people is that we have nothing to compare long-term relationships to, and there is a risk of feeling like our relationships are abnormal. Think about what I am saying. If we believe we *should* feel butterflies after ten years, we will wonder if there is something wrong with us, our partners, or our relationships when we don't. (Clue: If you are still feeling butterflies after ten years, see your physician. It may be something else.)

In some circumstances, you may not have an unhealthy relationship, and it may just be a matter of understanding normal developmental expectations. In other circumstances, things may have gone to shit. What I want to do is help you sort through fact vs. fiction.

While there will be some variation, it is not realistic to think your relationship won't change or that it will always be hot and heavy. Expectations like this will lead to predictable disappointment.

This begs some pretty important questions.

What is love? What does love feel like? What is a healthy relationship?

RELATIONSHIP FOUNDATIONS

We're going to that familiar place where we keep finding ourselves—childhood. I promise not to just blame your mother. Your father is also to blame.

The foundation for all relationships is built early in life, based on how caregivers treat us. Imagine if our needs are met, we are treated with love and respect, and we feel safe: we are much more likely to develop a sense of trust with others, and that serves as a reference point as we expand our relationships beyond parents and loved ones in the home. At the same time, however, we are using this data—how others treat us—to form our sense of self. In any relationship, there is ourself and there are others. We have an internal representation of ourselves and representations of others based on early life experiences. Both representations are forming at the same time and are related.

My favorite theory that illustrates self and other representations comes from Charles Cooley and is called Looking Glass Self.[14] Here is how it works. When a child looks into the faces of important others, that child sees a reflection of self. If the reflection is along the lines of *you are great; you are wonderful; I love you so much*, kids incorporate a sense of being lovable and important. If kids see a consistent reflection, the message is solid. But the opposite can also be true. A child can develop messages of not being okay or not being lovable. This all goes back to how core beliefs are formed.

This simple model explains how the early foundations of healthy relationships are developed, and they have everything to do with how we see ourselves. If we see ourselves as unworthy and unlovable, that will inform our relationship choices. If we have learned that others are inconsistent and untrustworthy, that will inform our relationship choices. All this also informs our definition of what love is and how it feels to be loved.

WHAT IS LOVE?

Some people really struggle with this question. Perhaps it is because they are looking for something black and white, something measurable. Maybe it is because what they experienced as a child didn't feel like love. Sometimes it is because they are looking for validation of their own feelings.

I will admit that this is a hard question that people ask me.

According to Dictionary.com (accessed 4/11/20)[15], love is "a profoundly tender, passionate affection for another person; a feeling of warm personal attachment or deep affection, as for a parent, child, or friend; sexual passion or desire."

When I read that, I think *Yeah. Whatever.* What rubs me the wrong way is that the definition doesn't really comment on what healthy love is in a relationship. I know the definition of love isn't meant to pass judgment on what is healthy, but this is so confusing to people. Love is love, right?

Not exactly.

Some people feel a deep sense of affection, but their affection is fucked up. It isn't what I would consider love, or at least healthy love. If someone feels so much affection that they want to rape you, is that love? If someone feels so much affection that they want to control your every move, is that love? I would argue it is not genuine love, and I know it isn't healthy love.

The problem is that if you have never experienced genuine love from a parent or caregiver, how are you supposed to know what healthy love in a relationship looks like?

To me, love (within a relationship) is a deep affection, and it comes with selflessness. What I mean by that is that when you really love someone, you so want what is best for that person that you sometimes put aside your own needs, and it isn't a big problem because the other person is doing the same thing for you. (Notice I said *sometimes*, which is not the same as having no boundaries as discussed in Chapter 7. This kind of selflessness *is* a problem.) Love involves respect. It takes trust and kindness into account. Love is safe and dangerous at the same time. It is safe because it is reciprocated. The other person is caring for you while you are caring for that person. It is dangerous because there is always an inherent risk of being hurt.

There are no guarantees in love. We are all humans. Humans change. Humans make mistakes. You can't help who you love, but you can help *how* you love—meaning the mere fact that you feel it doesn't mean you should take risks with your heart. The fact that you feel love doesn't mean that it is safe for you. Remember, feelings aren't always rational.

ABUSE: WHAT LOVE IS NOT

Interestingly, I feel like it is easier to talk about what love is not than what love is. Again, here, I am talking about what *healthy* love is not.

Healthy love is not abuse, no matter how you package it. So, what is abuse?

According to Dictionary.com,[15] abuse is "to use wrongly or improperly; to treat in a harmful, injurious, or offensive way; to speak insultingly, unjustly, or harshly to or about." I have been surprised that many people don't recognize abuse in their own relationships.

The purpose of abuse is to assert power and control over someone else through the application of pain, manipulation, and coercion.

In the 1980s, the Minnesota Domestic Abuse Intervention Programs developed the Power and Control Wheel to illustrate qualities of abuse in relationships. I have found this tool to be incredibly useful in working with those who have been abused. In a working session, I read the descriptors, and people self-assess. Every single time I have done this, the listeners have found it applicable to their relationships. They are typically surprised to learn that their relationships are abusive. It is new information.

POWER AND CONTROL WHEEL

Physical and sexual assaults, or threats to commit them, are the most apparent forms of domestic violence and are usually the actions that allow others to become aware of the problem. However, regular use of other abusive behaviors by the batterer, when reinforced by one or more acts of physical violence, make up a larger system of abuse. Although physical assaults may occur only once or occasionally, they instill threat of future violent attacks and allow the abuser to take control of the woman's life and circumstances.

The Power & Control diagram is a particularly helpful tool in understanding the overall pattern of abusive and violent behaviors, which are used by a batterer to establish and maintain control over his partner. Very often, one or more violent incidents are accompanied by an array of these other types of abuse. They are less easily identified, yet firmly establish a pattern of intimidation and control in the relationship.

VIOLENCE — physical — sexual

COERCION AND THREATS: Making and/or carrying out threats to do something to hurt her. Threatening to leave her, commit suicide, or report her to welfare. Making her drop charges. Making her do illegal things.

INTIMIDATION: Making her afraid by using looks, actions, and gestures. Smashing things. Destroying her property. Abusing pets. Displaying weapons.

MALE PRIVILEGE: Treating her like a servant: making all the big decisions, acting like the "master of the castle," being the one to define men's and women's roles.

EMOTIONAL ABUSE: Putting her down. Making her feel bad about herself. Calling her names. Making her think she's crazy. Playing mind games. Humiliating her. Making her feel guilty.

ECONOMIC ABUSE: Preventing her from getting or keeping a job. Making her ask for money. Giving her an allowance. Taking her money. Not letting her know about or have access to family income.

ISOLATION: Controlling what she does, who she sees and talks to, what she reads, and where she goes. Limiting her outside involvement. Using jealousy to justify actions.

USING CHILDREN: Making her feel guilty about the children. Using the children to relay messages. Using visitation to harass her. Threatening to take the children away.

MINIMIZING, DENYING, AND BLAMING: Making light of the abuse and not taking her concerns about it seriously. Saying the abuse didn't happen. Shifting responsibility for abusive behavior. Saying she caused it.

POWER AND CONTROL

VIOLENCE — physical — sexual

Developed by: Domestic Abuse Intervention Project 202 East Superior Street Duluth, MN 55802 218.722.4134

Produced and distributed by:

NATIONAL CENTER on Domestic and Sexual Violence training · consulting · advocacy 4612 Shoal Creek Blvd · Austin, Texas 78756 512.407.9020 (phone and fax) · www.ncdsv.org

This is printed with permission from the National Center on Domestic and Sexual Violence.[16]

The original Power and Control Wheel is dated, as it takes the perspective of traditional heterosexual relationships where the male is the abuser. I have actually worked with men who have been abused as well. I have also worked with non-heterosexual couples where abuse is prevalent. The original Power and Control Wheel has been adapted in numerous ways to be more inclusive and gen-

TEEN POWER AND CONTROL WHEEL

Produced and distributed by:

Developed from:
Domestic Abuse Intervention Project
202 East Superior Street
Duluth, MN 55802
218.722.4134

NATIONAL CENTER
on Domestic and Sexual Violence
training · consulting · advocacy
4612 Shoal Creek Blvd. · Austin, Texas 78756
512.407.9020 (phone and fax) · www.ncdsv.org

eralizable. Here, I include the additional versions for teens and lesbian, gay, and trans individuals. There are many other forms of the Power and Control Wheel in many other languages available on the NCDSV website. These are printed with permission from the National Center on Domestic and Sexual Violence.[16]

The power and control wheels include well-studied characteristics of abusive, controlling relationships. They are unhealthy, and they are not okay. Despite what you may have been told, you

Gay, Lesbian, Bisexual and Trans Power and Control Wheel

Developed by Roe & Jagodinsky

Adapted from the Power & Control and Equity Wheels developed by the
Domestic Abuse Intervention Project ● 206 West Fourth Street ● Duluth, Minnesota 55806 ● 218/722-4134

TEXAS COUNCIL ON FAMILY VIOLENCE

P.O. Box 161810 ● Austin, Texas 78716
Phone: 512/794-1133 ● Fax: 512/784-1199
www.tcfv.org

are *not* crazy if you object to being treated like shit. You may feel crazy because you know the relationship is messed up, but you are being told *you* are the problem. This is abuse.

As I mentioned earlier, recognizing abuse isn't so easy, particularly if it is all you have ever known in life. So be careful of being judgy here. Many people have grown up experiencing abuse from parents and other loved ones. These early life experiences may have created twisted core beliefs we may have about not being good enough or not deserving. Sometimes we may abuse ourselves as well, which makes it even harder to recognize when another person's behavior is inappropriate. For some people, it may seem *normal* or *expected* to be abused. Even so, abuse is not love.

Take a moment to really think about what I am saying. If you have never experienced a truly loving relationship—based on healthy love—how can you expect to be a good judge of it later in life? Romantic relationships can be more of the same.

I am not saying that people who have been abused do not know healthy love. I am saying that it can be more challenging if no one ever taught you healthy love.

When I meet someone in an abusive relationship, I often see all the shame and guilt they have about being in it. They worry about being judged. They may try to cover it up, excuse it, or explain it.

None of that here. Every one of us has the potential to be in an abusive relationship. It is not a matter of being stupid, needy, or lacking self-respect: it is a matter of being human.

I recognize when the person is engaging in self-blame and criticism about allowing it to happen. This is bullshit, and I like to get ahead of this by explaining the following:

I understand how abusive relationships typically begin. Things start as flattering. It feels so good to have someone who is so into you. Maybe he brings you flowers. Maybe he smothers you with compliments. Finally, you have found someone who is all about you. This progresses into him confessing all-passionate love, so much so that he wants to know everything about you: where you are, who you are with, and what you are doing all times. The abuser presents his behavior as flattering when it is really jealous and controlling. He twists his intentions and behaviors in ways that make you feel like you are the one with the problem. You doubt yourself. That is all part of the MO. People who abuse are drawn to people who are vulnerable (for whatever reason—low self-esteem to being extremely nice or people-pleasing) because they are easier to control. These people are less likely to walk away or set boundaries.

What can feel like intense love from another can easily turn into abuse, and there are many iterations to consider. Yet my point is very simple: abuse is not love. There is no justification for abuse. Abuse is never something that you cause another person to do, and it is never done out of love. If anyone tells you these things, they are lying to control you. You deserve better. You deserve more. You deserve to be safe in any relationship. No one, and I mean *no one* deserves abuse, and no one should suffer in a relationship because they feel they chose it. I write much more about how to get away from an abuser in chapter 6, as leaving can be dangerous. Just know you are not alone, and there *is* a way out.

· GETTING THERE ·

Take some time to think about what love means to you. Jot down some ideas about what elements of love are important to you. How have you compromised these ideals in the past? How do your early-life experiences and core beliefs affect how you view and experience love?

EXPECTATIONS OF LOVE

Now that you understand what love is and is not, let's move on to a better understanding of the expectations of love.

Robert Sternberg, Ph.D.,[17] is a preeminent developmental psychologist whose specialty is studying how humans change over time. He is an expert on love.

I'm guessing that before now, you haven't spent much time pondering how love develops and changes over time. We all like how it feels when love is going well, and we hate it when it isn't. Beyond knowing that, few people have spent time contemplating theories of love. I get why. It's a buzz kill.

Love feels so good when it is going well, it's almost like a drug. We shouldn't have to analyze it, right? I agree that love isn't something we can plan or even control. Love is a feeling. Feelings just happen. What I am saying is that we need to be smart about managing those feelings.

Knowing about the developmental trajectory and theory behind love will help us better understand ourselves and our reactions.

Think of it this way: I feel really, really good when I am eating a hot fudge brownie sundae. In fact, sometimes I feel like eating more than one. At the same time, I have to let logic kick in to remind me that the hangover or side effect from complete indulgence is feeling nasty and self-loathsome. It is an internal battle between feeling good and knowing that indulgence will sometimes have consequences. At the very least, I need to be honest about what those consequences are, rather than blindly indulging in the feel-good moment.

Okay, back to Sternberg. He has proposed a couple of theories: the Triangular Theory of Love, and the Theory of Love as a Story. He has now combined those two into the Duplex Theory of Love. I am going to break down each theory; but if you combine the two, you get the Duplex theory.[17]

THEORIES OF LOVE

Let's start with the **Triangular Theory**. According to this theory, love has three parts: **intimacy, passion,** and **decision/commitment.**

Intimacy: feelings of warmth, connection, and closeness. It is the experience of bonding.

Passion: feelings of intense arousal and attraction.

Decision/commitment: deciding on purpose to love someone even if the other person is not committed.

The three parts are separate, but they intermingle. For example, I may feel more passion as I become more intimate, which may then lead to a stronger commitment.

Some types of love in Triangular Theory include:

- **Passionate love** is associated with strong feelings of love and desire for a specific person. This love is full of excitement and newness. Passionate love is important in the beginning of the relationship and typically lasts for about a year. Passionate love comes with changes in the brain—specifically, the increased feel-good neurotransmitters that give a sensation equivalent to feeling high. While this kind of love feels great, it is important to remember that the physiological feeling cannot last.

- **Companionate love** follows passionate love. Companionate love is also known as affectionate love. When a couple reaches this level of love, they feel mutual understanding and care for each other. This type of love helps relationships survive longer-term. It comes later on in the relationship and requires a certain level of knowledge for each person in the relationship. (Example: Benny and Lorenzo have companionate love.)

- **Non-love** is the absence of all three components. There are several other combinations listed below.
- **Liking** is when only intimacy is present.
- **Infatuation** is when only passion is present.
- **Empty Love** is when only decision/commitment is present.
- **Romantic Love** is when intimacy and passion are present.
- **Fatuous Love** is when passion and decision/commitment are present.
- **Consummate Love** is when all three components of love are present.

If we think of the three components of love as representing a triangle, the balance of the triangle depends on the balance of the three components. A balanced triangle is equilateral, but there may be many different forms.

Sternberg also states that there may be a triangle for what is actually present, and a different triangle for the love a person wishes were present. This is what I call the fairy tale. It is when there is reality, but the person has an idea of what it *could be* if only . . . the other person would change, we lived somewhere else, we had kids, etc.

The separate triangle for the love the person wishes were present is so hard for most people to get over. People aren't grieving the fucked-up relationship they have. They are grieving the amazing relationship they *could have* had. People get stuck in bad relationships because of a fear of missing out on a change (for the better) that never comes. Alternatively, they may be struggling to get over relationships they've lost but never really existed in the first place.

The **Love as a Story theory** represents the scripts we bring into relationships. This idea ties directly back to our core beliefs about love and relationships. Love as a Story suggests that we all have a life story that affects how we see the world. (Think of those filters we talked about earlier.) Sternberg states that we are likely to be more successful in relationships with others who fit with our storylines.

Makes sense, right? We are looking for the other characters in our already pre-written stories. This is why it is so important that we recognize when our stories are fucked up, because we will choose fucked-up characters to match. The other person in the relationship is doing the same thing.

Sternberg provides a list of popular storylines from literature, movies, and popular culture, but the list could be endless, and I describe some of them here. I'm sure you can think of some on your own.

- **Addiction:** When a person becomes clingy and is paralyzed by thoughts of fear of losing the relationship.
- **Art:** When a person is more concerned about how their partner looks or how physically attractive the partner is.
- **Business:** When the relationship is more of a business arrangement.
- **Collection:** When the partner is seen as more of an object that fits with other parts of life.
- **Cookbook:** When a person sees a relationship as needing to follow a certain recipe in order to be considered a success.
- **Fantasy:** This is the fairytale . . . the princess-and-the-frog or white-knight tale.
- **Game:** The relationship is seen as more of a game or sport.
- **Gardening:** The idea that relationships must be tended like a garden.
- **Government:** Relationships have a model where decisions are either autocratic or democratic.

- **History:** A record of the relationship's history is always kept.
- **Horror:** Relationships include elements of terror or horror.
- **Humor:** Love is kind of strange and humorous.
- **Mystery:** Relationships need to involve some mystery. One should not reveal too much.
- **Police:** It is important to police your partner to make sure they are on good behavior.
- **Pornography:** Love is dirty.
- **Religion:** Love is dictated by religious beliefs.
- **Science:** Love can be studied, analyzed, and predicted.
- **Sacrifice:** Love means giving of oneself.
- **Theater:** Love is scripted.
- **Travel:** Love is a journey.
- **War:** Love is a battlefield.

The idea is that we all have stories about ourselves that our caregivers started crafting about us when we were born. The stories may also include the example set by our parents and how they showed love to one another. It is those core beliefs and other ideas about ourselves that we developed. We are looking for information that fits with our stories as we grow older, which includes relationships. We are drawn to others who support our stories.

Why do I share all this with you? Because it is incredibly important that we know ourselves. We need to know our own storylines or core beliefs that drive us to behave in certain ways, because we will do this over and over, even if it is not in our best interest. We may be drawn to storylines that are familiar, but it doesn't mean they are healthy for us.

We need to understand that love is a feeling, but it has important cognitive components. It can be helpful to evaluate our experiences in terms of science so we are not just swept up in feelings.

We need to remind ourselves that feelings are best interpreted within a context.

Emotions like passion can easily overcome gut instincts or better judgment. Sometimes a strong need for intimacy can override the facts about decision/commitment that are also important.

· *GETTING THERE* ·

Spend some time writing about what storylines seem to fit for you. How have you been drawn to certain characters in relationships? How has this worked out? What are the needs that seem to drive you? How can you channel this energy into something that is a healthy fit?

WHAT IS NORMAL?

I once had someone consult me for fear that maybe he should end his marriage. He said his wife was a good person. They were friends. He liked her, but she did get on his nerves. They got along well, with some arguments. They didn't have sex every day (or twice on good days) like they used to, and generally the passion had declined. They were both tired a lot, with the kids and all. Since this was his only marriage, he thought maybe the situation was not good. He was sure others were having more sex than he was. He thought he was supposed to be completely fulfilled by his marriage and wondered if, because he was not, maybe he should get out and find fulfillment in another relationship. This guy was completely confused.

When he looked on social media, he knew his marriage wasn't all the diamonds and roses he saw others portray. When

I explained that his situation didn't seem abnormal, he seemed so relieved. However, I wasn't saying that relationships get stale, and he just had to accept it. We all have to work at it. I was just saying it is not appropriate to expect that this guy's relationship with his wife would always be in the hot-and-heavy-honeymoon stage.

And I imagined his wife had to be thanking me. She was too tired to think about sex twice a day.

If you look at the research on marital satisfaction, it's easy to get confused. Even the experts don't seem to agree. Some believe satisfaction starts high, declines, and then goes back up. Others believe it just goes down. Still others believe that it goes up and down sporadically.

Currently, the divorce rate is somewhere between 40 and 50 percent of all first marriages, which is down from a high of 60 percent a few decades ago.[18] At the same time, the marriage rate is also going down, meaning that fewer people are deciding to get married in the first place.

Here is a way to think about it, whether you marry or not. When we first enter into a relationship, we are passionate and aroused (Sternberg's passionate love), and the excitement and newness may lead to a feeling similar to being *high on love*. We may share goals and ideas for the future and become consumed in making future plans. The *work* of the relationship doesn't feel like work. There is a lot of time spent building intimacy, because there is a lot of free time available, and it feels so good.

At some point life takes over, and we get overwhelmed by careers, bills, and raising children if we decide to have them. It is very easy to stop putting in the time, because we are tired and there are many competing priorities. It is easy to become disconnected and distant. Then there is simple aging. We get tired more easily. Everything seems to take more energy. When their children leave home, couples can feel like they have lost common ground, lost intimacy, and lost connections.

This seems like a downer, right? It isn't meant to be. It is a hard truth that flies in the face of the fairy tales we have all been told, which seem to be a key part of the problem in relationships after all. That is, relationships take work. Happy endings come after a lot of effort. There will be ups and downs. While it won't always be pleasant, I do think there is some comfort in knowing the general trajectory of human relationships. There is a predictable pattern.

LOVE TAKES WORK

We may tell ourselves love should just happen if it is right. Love shouldn't be work. If love is meant to be, it works out. This is kind of true, at least in the beginning. I generally tell people that the first year of a relationship should be like a honeymoon. Too much fighting isn't a good sign. And, after that first year, people start to let their guards down because the love potion is wearing off. This is when you begin to see reality, if you are open to it.

Early love should be easy.

Long-term, however, staying in love takes a lot of effort, especially when the feel-good brain chemicals wear off. Then we are faced with the sober truth that we have many other commitments and responsibilities, and that our partner can truly be annoying.

If we have the unrealistic expectation that we should always be on top of the world in relationships or things will always be wonderful, we will be sadly mistaken. Relationships will grow and transform over time, just as we grow and transform over time as individuals. While passionate love may be where things started, companionate love may be where things grow. That doesn't mean the passion is gone and it's a sign to go out and find new love. Most all relationships move past passionate love. It is basic behaviorism that we habituate, and what was once new becomes old and familiar.

We need to consider all this within the context of our core beliefs and the things we tell ourselves. It is important to understand oneself alone before understanding oneself in a relationship. It is also essential to choose wisely. It can be easy to get caught up in the emotions of the moment without considering our long-term tendencies.

For example, some people become passionate about being with someone who has an opposite personality. It is like being on a quest to complete oneself. Be careful of looking for *you complete me* in another person. Only *you* can complete yourself. Anything else is a lie.

JED AND RASHIDA'S STORY

Jed is an introvert and tends to be very low-key. He is a planned, organized, and incredibly neat introvert who tends to be very low-key. Rashida is highly extroverted, spontaneous, risk-taking, and energetic. At first, Jed and Rashida feel highly attracted to one another, but in the long term they drive each other insane. Each is who they are. Neither is right or wrong. Despite initial attraction, in order to be successful in love there needs to be a level of honesty regarding how well the other person will fit with your personality, values, and lifestyle.

These are the people I see in couples counseling, and it is difficult for me because each is a cool person in their own right. I think we all admire qualities in another person that perhaps we wish we ourselves had—but we also have to be honest about who we are, not who we want to be. The point I am making is we have to be honest about what we bring to the table and honest about how opposite personalities will actually mesh in real life. The essential question is: Are we looking to fix something within ourselves by choosing a certain partner who is different?

HOW DO I AVOID REPEATING PAST MISTAKES?

One thought triggers a lot of people who are recovering from the loss of a relationship: *What if I make the same mistakes again?* You can see how fear could get in the way of healing. There are times when this is an unfounded fear because of a bad relationship, and there are other times when there is evidence of an unhealthy pattern. Either way, I recommend something that involves getting into your head and being intentional.

One of the tried and true ways I encourage people to be intentional about relationships is to get a sheet of paper and make three columns. The first column should be a comprehensive list of things you absolutely must have in a relationship. These are things you should not and will not compromise. This may include things like having a job, sharing certain values, being neat, or being a certain age. Again, at this point, it is essential that people be honest with themselves, because we all have certain drives toward what is familiar but may not be healthy.

MANUEL'S STORY

Manuel has a pattern of choosing to date people who are emotional roller coasters. They start off very passionately, but seemingly out of the blue the people begin to attack him and create drama. Manuel never sees it coming. He's too caught up in the passion.

It isn't as if I would tell Manuel to avoid passion, because it is, after all, one of the corners of the love triangle. Rather, I would tell him he needs to look for other signs that might predict stability in a partner. Folks in Manuel's position typically tell me they are so worried about missing the signs and making the same mistakes that in the end they consider not dating at all. I tell them I cannot guarantee any particular outcomes, but a certain strategy might help reduce the chance of choosing another emotionally unstable partner.

Manuel's must-have list should probably include things like: must have excellent family relationships and a good childhood, must have a history of stable long-term relationships, and must have a low-key personality. Again, while these qualities do not rule out emotionally unstable partners, it reduces the likelihood of repeating past patterns. However, the onus is upon Manuel to make his list and to stick to it.

The second column to add to your document is a list of things one must *not* have in a relationship, which might include drug, tobacco, or alcohol use, children from a previous marriage, significant debt, etc.

And the third column is a list of things that don't really matter, like hair or eye color, occupation, income, etc.

Once you have these three lists that were intentionally based on your past patterns, true desires, and personality, it is your job to not deviate from them. This document is something you can use as a guide or road map. When you meet someone interesting, before you go off into fairy-tale land where passion overtakes good sense, you should check to see if the person meets your criteria. If the person doesn't meet your black-and-white, yes-or-no criteria, there is no need to continue interacting. Further interactions will only lead to shades of gray and confusion, where one convinces oneself that the list doesn't matter, or that it is all in the way you see it. Further interactions with this person will lead to deviation from your stated values.

In MOMF lingo, it is knowing your bullshit history, calling yourself out on the bullshit, and being smarter than your bullshit so you can keep yourself in line.

Think of it this way: We make plans for education, for careers, and for life in general. Why not make a plan about something as important as finding love? I'll tell you why most people don't: because we have been taught that love is something you fall into. The implication (and indeed, the suggestion) is that you lose your common sense and stop thinking. While this may be true early on due to attraction, I am suggesting that you re-engage your head in the conversation.

In the end, successful love is just like most success in life: it is bringing your head in alongside your heart. It is using both to lead you to the right place. You. You can't help feeling what you feel, but you shouldn't always act on that. Successful love depends a great deal on how well you know yourself, your drives, your strengths, and your weaknesses. It is also how well you manage this information to make good decisions in your life. However, even doing all of this well doesn't guarantee a good outcome. We are all on this crazy journey together. Every experience we have is an opportunity to learn, but we have to be willing and able to sort it out without judgment and see what makes sense. Love is also about patience and stamina. Loving relationships do change over time. People change over time. Those are givens in the equation. Change isn't good or bad: it just *is*.

Instead of being reactive, however, we need to step back and decide what to do with the information. Just because we don't understand it doesn't mean it is bad: it means we need to observe and be open. We are all motherfuckers on that bus.

· *GETTING THERE* ·

Get into your head and do the three-column exercise. When you think of past relationships, what core beliefs and self-talk drove your decisions? What gaps were you seeking to fill? What advice would you give to your younger self, based on what you know now? What are the pitfalls you need to flag? What will you do with this information?

6

No, You Didn't!

Amita and Ivy were known to their friends as *the soul sisters*. They did everything together. They'd lived together for ten years, moving in right after they'd started dating. They opted not to get married, because everyone knew they were committed; but they lived like a married couple.

They were also very socially active. They were in the golf league, the basketball league, the softball league. They had an extensive community network and were both socially extroverted.

Sometimes it was hard to tell that Amita and Ivy were romantically involved, because they acted more like buddies, but they saw this as an evolution of their relationship. They were, after all, the best of friends. Neither thought this was an issue, and no one complained.

Enter Tim. Tim worked at the same place as Ivy, but they were in separate departments. Due to downsizing, the two departments merged, and Tim and Ivy were put on the same project. No biggie. Except that Ivy began to talk more and more about Tim. She didn't hide her friendship with him. In fact, she was quite open about it, so Amita didn't think much of the talk between the two.

She certainly wasn't jealous. Tim was a guy, and Ivy wasn't into guys. He wasn't a threat, and the friendship wasn't a threat.

Then Ivy needed to work on projects with Tim more and more, and this cut into after-work activities like golf and softball. Amita began to feel suspicious. When she would bring it up with Ivy, Ivy would minimize the situation. Ivy would tell Amita she was being controlling and over the top. Amita would lay off for a while, but her gut told her something was off. She couldn't point her finger at it. It was an intuition thing.

Amita was ready to hire a private detective when she received a phone call one evening from a woman who claimed to be Tim's wife. This woman viciously poured out all of the details of the infidelity between Ivy and Tim. Amita wanted to hang up and stop the barrage. She wanted to pretend it wasn't happening. But at the same time, she paradoxically felt unable to stop listening. It was as if she was being validated—that she wasn't crazy or losing her mind. At the same time, she was hearing her world coming to an end.

When Ivy came home, Amita confronted her, and she initially denied everything. She said Tim's wife was a nut job who was trying to create drama. Ivy spun an intricate yarn to explain away all of Amita's fears and accusations. Amita felt a mixture of disbelief and relief. She didn't want any of it to be true, but at the same time, her gut told her that no part of the explanation was true.

She just couldn't shake the feeling that things were amiss.

Amita followed up with a private investigator, and she received rock-solid visual evidence that Ivy was cheating on her. Again, she had mixed feelings of relief that she wasn't being a complete paranoid bitch, alongside feelings of utter devastation and betrayal.

Amita confronted Ivy again with the evidence. This time she caved and admitted the infidelity. Unfortunately, Ivy did not stop there. She went on to share that she was in love with Tim *and* with Amita. She didn't want to choose.

Ivy portrayed herself as a victim who needed pity for being in such a terrible position. Like one would do with a friend, Ivy shared her innermost feelings of affection for Tim. She told Amita about what drew her to him in contrast to her long-lasting relationship with Amita. Ivy highlighted the things about Amita that drove her crazy, as if to justify her infidelity. She also shared that she didn't want to lose her house, her standard of living, and her social network if she left Amita for Tim.

Ivy overshared.

At some point, Amita felt like her soul was leaving her body. She was in the room but couldn't be fully present, because the situation was unreal. The love of her life was telling her all about being in love with someone else. Ivy seemed to expect that Amita was going to feel sorry for her. Amita was not capable at that moment of making any sense out of the conversation, and she couldn't stop herself from asking more questions. She found herself insisting that Ivy tell her intimate details of the sexual relationship between herself and Tim. She insisted on knowing every lie, every infidelity. It was both excruciating and irresistible. Looking back, Amita knew that had been a mistake. This created unforgettable images in her mind.

After several marathon conversations that led nowhere new, Ivy said she "could not" choose who she wanted to be with. She asked if she could continue living in the house and see where things went. Amita was repulsed by this idea, but she was similarly repulsed by the idea of saying good-bye to Ivy. Now Amita felt stuck.

This was a shit sandwich. Should she take a bite?

Amita consulted me to ask this question: "What do you think I should do?"

I know two things at this point:

1) She knows what to do, but she doesn't want to do it.

2) She isn't looking for another person to tell her what to do. What Amita is seeking instead is the answer to this question: *Can Ivy be fixed so that we can go back to the way it was?*

If I tell Amita that Ivy can be fixed, she will feel better about a decision to stick it out with her. If Ivy cannot be fixed, she will have faith in her decision to leave Ivy. Amita is looking for support and justification, but she is focused on variables that are outside of her control, which leaves her completely vulnerable to ongoing hurt.

THE WICKED AND THE FUCKED

I have heard multiple variations on this story many times. My internal response is generally the same and consists of lengthy, indecipherable spews of profanity, which are inappropriate to share with a patient. When I eventually open my mouth, I communicate this message in some way: "You deserve to be with someone who knows she wants to be with you."

I don't see all infidelity through the same lens. If the person who was unfaithful admits to being unfaithful, asks for forgiveness, and asks for help, this is workable. In this scenario, the unfaithful person takes responsibility and chooses a side. I can work with that.

The problem with Amita's story and so many others is that there is the crippling pain of learning that a partner is unfaithful— *and* lopped on top is having to process the insulting indecision of the partner. Sometimes, for an extra dose of pain, the person who is unfaithful blames the partner for the infidelity. "So, I admit that I cheated on you. I don't know if I am sorry for it. I am not sure if I want to be with you or the other person. And, I'm kinda thinking it's your fault that this happened." Talk about a triple-decker shit sandwich.

And before you get all judgy, thinking you would never put up with that bullshit, hit the pause button. Everyone seems to know how they would handle it—until it happens to them. Feelings change everything. Plus, every human being out there has the capacity to be unfaithful. Those are the facts.

What is unacceptable, however, is the unbelievable selfishness of holding the person who has been cheated on hostage to indecision or finger-pointing. This is where it is so important to protect oneself. The problem is that people who have been cheated on may be so shell-shocked from discovering the affair that it is hard to have any perspective. Talk to a friend. Talk to a therapist. Talk to someone who will listen and not tell you what to do—but will remind you to self-protect.

As I have already said, infidelity is something all humans are capable of, and by itself it does not necessarily signal the end of a relationship. There are a lot of factors that go into deciding if a relationship is worth salvaging. If you are reading this book, I will assume your relationship is over or pretty darn close. Perhaps you are on the continuing journey of trying to understand or validate that you have done the right thing.

The reason this chapter is important is not to focus on the past for the sake of re-analyzing it all. No, what is crucial is that you learn from the past and grow from it. The ultimate tragedy would be allowing infidelity to become a cancer in your mind that takes over all future relationships without cause. The ultimate tragedy would be allowing someone else's infidelity to take away your trust in people. While the infidelity wasn't your choice, what you do with it is. That is what you can control, and that is on you. What will you do with it?

UNDERSTANDING INFIDELITY

Fidelity means being true or loyal to another person. Therefore, infidelity is being untrue or disloyal. When I talk about infidelity, I am talking about being unfaithful in the broad sense. It doesn't just mean having sex outside of a relationship. In fact, I find it easier to work with infidelity if it is just sex, because emotions don't play a primary role in that. And emotions fuck it all up.

Infidelity can also mean being emotionally intimate with someone outside of a committed relationship. I can be emotionally intimate with a good friend, but that is not what I am talking about; I am talking about the infidelity where one person in a committed relationship becomes emotionally entangled and attracted to another person around intimate personal issues. The person who is unfaithful steps outside of the committed relationship to share personal and emotional experiences with someone other than the committed partner. The shared connection leads to attraction, whether or not it is acted upon. This can happen with or without sexual activity accompanying it.

Emotional infidelity is much, much harder to repair, because humans can't just shut off feelings and emotions. You *can* stop having sex.

When I talk about infidelity in this section, I am referring to any infidelity.

There are multiple reasons for infidelity. I am going to cover some of the most common explanations. I want you to think of it along a risk-stratification spectrum. Any time we enter into a relationship, there is risk. Don't start a relationship telling yourself *This person would never cheat on me*. That just isn't true. It is also false to claim *Everyone will cheat on me*. The risk of infidelity ranges from low to high. Your job is to be an accurate judge so you are protected.

This section is also about understanding what can be fixed and what cannot. So let me give you some things to consider.

Basic Infidelity. Most commonly, infidelity occurs because of something missing in a relationship. A typical scenario is when a couple has been together for a very long time, and things get stale. Early on in relationships, we have those butterflies. We go the extra mile to make the other person feel special and wanted. Hygiene is important. We listen to every word like it is crucial. After a while, this gets old. It's a lot of work. We get distracted. We have other demands on us. We don't have the time or energy. We're human. When people stop working on the relationship, it leaves room for vulnerability. People who have unmet needs (whether they know it or not) are susceptible to having those needs met outside of the relationship.

This type of infidelity absolutely can be fixed, as long as both parties are willing to accept responsibility for their part. Take a moment. This can be hard to hear. Both parties have a responsibility. I know it is incredibly hard to hear that the person who was cheated on has responsibility; but once the air clears, it becomes easier to see. This is not victim-blaming. I said both parties have some responsibility, and this does not excuse the fact that the person who cheated made the unfortunate decision to step out of the relationship.

Sometimes counseling is needed to heal, to identify what went wrong, and to organize a plan for change. Sometimes counseling isn't needed. It is more a matter of learning from what went wrong and developing a sustained plan to address the gaps.

Mismatches. This type of infidelity comes about when two people aren't meant to be together because they are just too different. They are mismatches, and this leads to stepping outside of the relationship due to different values, different interests, or different personality styles. Some difference is good, but too much creates vulnerability. This is not fixable. Each person is a unique self. Even if they want to change, it will not be permanent. Acceptance of this is disappointing because there may be desire there, but it denies reality.

Open Relationships. This part may be confusing. You can have infidelity among people in open relationships or people who swing. I want to say at the outset that I am biased against these relationships. Perhaps it is because I only see the ones that don't work. I am referring to couples where two people are in a committed relationship, but one or both have sex with others with the consent of both parties. Sometimes the sex with others involves both partners, with one or more parties. Sometimes the sex with others is both partners having separate relationships with other people. Sometimes it's about one of the partners having sex with other people. These are the variations I have seen, but I am sure there are many others. Regardless, in my experience, the relationships seem to end up in an ugly place. One person falls in love with someone outside of the committed relationship. One person starts lying. Boundaries are crossed. People develop unexpected intimacies and connections in relationships that were supposed to be casual.

I get it. In theory, if two people in a committed relationship both agree to have sexual relations outside of the committed relationship, it should work, right? In my view, this completely ignores the fact that human beings are not black and white. Human beings are full of confusing, irrational emotions that don't fit theory. Put several humans together in a messy situation, and shit happens that no one is prepared for but everyone should expect.

I am not saying folks shouldn't be in open relationships. I am just saying I don't think they work long-term, and someone generally gets hurt. Think about the risk stratification and at least be honest about it. That is the more important point.

Infidelity in open relationships can be fixed by ending open relationships. It is drastically reducing the risk of infidelity by eliminating the accepted presence of another party. Of course, both people have to agree to this, and there has to be a level of trust that the agreement is pure. Though I am not an expert on this area, I am not clear about how to continue in an open relationship and manage infidelity risk in a way that is healthy.

One Person Invited Someone with Deeper Problems to Couple. Last but not least, you have relationships that include someone with a more deeply damaged psyche. These are the people I address in greater depth in chapter 7. I consider infidelity due to a person with a damaged psyche to be the exception, rather than the rule. Infidelity is usually due to more mundane explanations, like boredom.

So, who do I include in this last category? It's out there.

This category is reserved for times when the infidelity is actually due to the fault of one person. It is clearly obvious that one person in the committed relationship acted out inappropriately because of internal, dysfunctional factors. You have folks with sex addictions, chronic liars, narcissists, folks with no empathy or conscience, and folks who have an excessive need for attention. For the most part, I do not believe this category is fixable with the exception of someone who has a sex addiction. I do believe sex addictions are treatable if the person who has the addiction is committed to change. I do not include sex addictions in chapter 7, because the chapter is reserved for the people who I do not believe are capable of significant change.

DISTORTED EXPLANATIONS

Commonly, people who have been cheated on prefer to look for sexy reasons for infidelity. I see folks who have detailed explanations for why the spouse cheated as they try to convince me that their situation is exceptional. I understand this is because no one wants to believe the person she loves could do this. It hurts too damned bad. These people still have one foot in the denial stage.

They look for the exception to the *equation*, not to the rule. What I mean is that it is common to believe that some slut, tart, sex-starved man-whore wormed their way into the partner's mind—taking it over, brainwashing the partner. The partner somehow was mentally weak and fell prey to the mind control, thus hypnotically cooperating. This is a cop-out. The person who cheated knowingly did so as a competent, complicit adult. It is easier to blame the person he cheated with, but this isn't about ease.

Another explanation I see is when the person who has been cheated on believes she somehow pushed the other person into cheating: the infidelity is her fault. I mean, if she had just worn slutty lingerie every Friday night. If she'd only been more open to porn. If she'd only lost ten pounds, used Botox, and had a boob job. Nope. This is a cop-out too. A partner's infidelity has everything to do with the partner and her choices. The partner could just as easily have left the relationship or had a crucial conversation. She is responsible for how she chose to handle things. Do not fall into the trap of giving anyone a break or a pass.

The explanations we create for infidelities often go back to our own core beliefs. Even if we are aware that our core beliefs are messed up, during times of stress we revert back to the baggage. So if we have beliefs that we are *not good enough* or *unlovable*, we may see the infidelity as proof of these beliefs. We may have beliefs that others are untrustworthy, and the current situation may seemingly prove that as well.

Beware. Our core beliefs can be distorted and dysfunctional. When we filter data through these lenses, it may appear to fit with what we think we know about the world, ourselves, and others—

but remember, the filter is biased. Catch the resulting negative self-talk of *I am doomed; I can't take this; No one will ever be faithful to me; This is all my fault*. It's not reality, and listening to it will make you feel insane.

What I want you to remember is that staying in a relationship where you don't trust the other person is doomed. And why would you want that, anyway? Ask yourself if you honestly trust the other person to have your back. Listen to your gut. You should not have to force a relationship. You cannot force someone to be faithful. You deserve better. Better is available.

· GETTING THERE ·

What core beliefs do you have that affect your understanding of infidelity in the relationship? What automatic thoughts are related to this? Ask yourself if the thoughts are helpful. Is there something you have done wrong? Most of the time, both of these answers are "no." Think about trust for a bit. Are you telling yourself that if you work hard to control all the variables at play, you will be safe? How is that going for you? What are you losing in the process?

GETTING BETTER

I find that the pain of being betrayed is so overwhelming that people cannot even think straight. The first hours and days are merely survival. Thoughts bounce back and forth between *This can't be true* and *This is so fucking true*. Emotions are on a roller coaster. (See chapter 3.)

If the relationship is not workable, it should become all about self-protection. Above all else, this is the best time to surround yourself with people who love you—family and friends. These people need to be the ones who are reining it in too. You don't want or need any I-told-you-so's. You don't need to feel judged or minimized. What you need is to have friends who will help the pain subside. These are people who will drag you out of bed and out to lunch even when you try to say no. They will take you to exercise class and get you to smile. They will kick your ass when you want to call your ex and cave. You want friends and family who will help you heal through love and acceptance. You want people who will call out the bullshit explanations and thoughts you generate to make it go away.

Don't lock yourself away. Life will seem different in the sunlight. Get out of bed. Do *not* contact your ex. It is like breathing in toxicity. Now is the time for healing.

Also, don't spend time investigating the person your partner was unfaithful with. There is nothing you will learn that will help you better understand yourself. I know some people obsess over knowing details about the other person, as if they will somehow discover something they are missing or can fix about themselves. *There is nothing to be found there*. Let that shit go.

Okay, I recognize that letting shit go isn't so easy, even though I want it to be.

While I genuinely believe that there is nothing healthy to be found there, I also recognize that most human beings cannot let it go. Most human beings want to know more. That is natural. That is normal. My fear, however, is that people will get into comparisons like *What does she have that I don't have?* Unfortunately, the focus of the infidelity can shift from the partner to the other person or, even worse, to beating oneself up. When I say "Let that shit go," I'm trying to protect you; but it is a necessary stop on some folks' journey.

Some people need to see and process the cold, hard facts in order to come to grips with an ugly reality. Details about the other person and how deeply the affair went may solidify certain truths that you'd been unwilling to see.

I will caution you, however, that if you proceed down the path of investigating details, you need to be honest with yourself. You may find out more than you wanted to know. The pain will be brutal. Maybe have a friend go on that journey with you to make sure you stay on course and help you process what you find— and, again, be careful about going down the path of comparisons. The greatest tragedy would be if you used what you find to feel worse about yourself.

While I still don't recommend getting into the weeds regarding the infidelity because the risk is so high, I respect and honor that some people may still need to do that as they move along the path to acceptance. Just be smart about it. Go in with your eyes open.

Remember that the reason someone cheats has something to do with the person who cheated and/or the relationship, not the person who was cheated on. Even if the person who was cheated on was a complete asshole, the choice to cheat is on the person who cheated. It wasn't that the asshole caused the cheating. None of us has that kind of mind or behavior control.

There is no need to continue having ongoing conversations about the infidelity once the decision has been made to end the relationship. What would be the point? Again, move on, motherfucker.

It is time to begin looking forward. What can you learn? Where do you go from here? How would you like your life to be different? And I hope you don't say that everyone cheats. Just like I believe we all have the potential to cheat, I also believe cheating isn't inevitable. Human beings do have a frontal lobe—the ability to do the adult thing—and the ability to say no. Relationships take a shit ton of work, and that work is endless. It's not always fun, but that does not equal infidelity.

On the other side of an infidelity experience, it is my hope that people do not incorporate distorted messages about themselves and carry garbage into future relationships. That just isn't fair to anyone. This takes a lot of reflection and work. This is a great time for journaling, which will help you organize your thoughts and gain perspective over time. In the end, I am guessing you will come to a sense that you are glad to put the asshole in the rearview mirror.

· GETTING THERE ·

After the pain of infidelity starts to subside, things are a lot more clear to analyze. What did you learn that will be of value to you in future relationships? How will you choose to allow the experience to affect you going forward? Write about it—all of it.

RECOMMENDED READING

Spring, Janis A. *After the Affair.* New York: HarperCollins, 2012.

7

Handling Extremely Bad Actors

There is the mindfuck of a breakup. Then there is the mindfuck of a breakup involving a bad actor. When relationships and breakups involve these folks, things can get beyond messy. The pain may be supercharged, and the agony is seemingly endless. This is because you are dealing with someone who is incredibly troubled and damaged. An easy exit is not going to happen. What I can do, though, is help you navigate the minefield of breaking up with someone who is more challenging than your average asshole.

This chapter is focused on the bad actors in breakups, including the narcissist, the dependent, the sociopath, the abuser, and the threatener.

Unlike other chapters in this book, this one looks at the breakup from the perspective of your wanting to get away from these bad actors. The feelings may be mixed—meaning that part of you may want to get away, and another part may want to stay. In the end, however, this chapter leans toward the idea that you know you need to be far, far away from these flawed individuals. The goal is to help you clearly see you aren't losing your mind and to develop the self-protection skills necessary to get you MOMF'ing in one piece.

THE NARCISSIST

Tylissa was stunningly beautiful, and when she met Gene, he was taken aback with how casually confident she was in her own skin. He was used to women being much more outwardly insecure. He felt so lucky to be with Tylissa that he gave her everything. He doted on her as though she were a rare, vintage treasure. She ate it up and seemingly always wanted more, which Gene was happy to provide. This was fine for a while, but then she began to criticize him more and more for what he was not giving her and not doing for her. Her thirst for praise and attention seemed unending. Whenever he would bring up his own needs, she would quickly turn the conversation back to her own concerns. Tylissa seemed untouched and unmoved by the stresses Gene faced or resources he lacked. It was as if she were unable to see beyond her own desires.

Gene noticed that she had begun to become too busy for him. She was going out with friends and showing off new things she got from God only knew where. Eventually, a horrified Gene found out that she was cheating on him. He had financially over-extended himself to keep her in new clothes and jewelry. He had high credit-card debt because he rarely said no to her requests, and she seemed oblivious to his limits. To top it off, Tylissa was put out that Gene was making a big deal out of her seeing some-one else. Did he not understand that she was too special to be tied down by his mediocrity? She blamed him for not living up to her expectations with no regard for how he felt. She chewed him up and spit him out. He was broken.

As he was licking his wounds, Tylissa would call or stop by as if they were still dating. She would expect him to dote on her, and she would slide in put-downs between all kinds of confusing messages. Gene was flabbergasted. He was very happy to see her, but he felt hatred building at the same time. He felt like he was losing it.

Breakups are horrible at baseline, but breaking up with a narcissist is like a nuclear explosion, especially if you are doing the breaking-up. This is because narcissists are highly, highly skilled at defense. Nothing sticks. And narcissists can't tolerate the idea that you are rejecting them. They have to make it about you.

Narcissists are experts at charm and manipulation. They are adept at fooling people with falsehoods. They can twist the truth so much that it is no longer recognizable. In fact, most people who are involved with narcissists question themselves to the point of insanity.

The narcissist is so good at manipulating facts that those around them doubt themselves and their own grasp on reality. This is all because narcissists cannot under any circumstances accept blame. It simply isn't possible. It doesn't compute. They are so good at deflecting that nothing sinks in. You can toss a ball that way, but it will be hit back to you so fast and hard that you may never even see it coming.

Narcissists and the other bad actors are experts at gaslighting as a means of abuse and control. Gaslighting is the phrase used to describe when another person tells repeated, false, deeply hurtful stories that destroy another person's reputation. The stories are told enough and with enough vigor that even the person being gaslighted may begin to believe the stories may be true. It is a tried-and-true strategy for narcissists to fuck with your mind.

For example, a person may be told over and over by a narcissist that she is crazy. The narcissist also tells this same story to other people. After a while, the person who is being told these things begins to believe it is true, despite its being made up as a means of abuse.

Hear this very clearly: If you have been taken in by a narcissist, it does not mean you are weak or gullible. It doesn't mean you are an idiot or naïve. Narcissists can be quite charming, which is why they are able to gain traction with other people. They are intuitively able to size people up and prey upon their vulnerabilities. They are adept at making people feel understood at a level that they have not previously felt understood. For brief periods of time, narcissists are able to convey a deep sense of connection as part of their overall drive to manipulate others. Narcissists are intuitively able to identify others' sensitive areas and exploit them.

I do not believe all narcissists set out to exploit others. In other words, I do not believe all narcissists consciously say to themselves "I will do this, this, and this to use other people." They just do it automatically. It is in their makeup. They don't know how not to do it. Using others is about narcissists' incessant, irretrievable drive to get what they want at all costs. They are just doing what they know how to do. That doesn't make it right or okay. My point, in case you are wondering, is *no, they will not change.*

I will say it again: narcissists will not change. Why is this point so important? Because some people think the narcissist can get professional help to become a better person. Unfortunately, this will not work. Yes, the narcissist may go to therapy after an ultimatum from a partner, but the point of the therapy will end up being how to cope with the person who is nagging, the person driving him crazy, the bitch. The narcissist will be telling the therapist how "the bitch" is doing things that cause him to act badly. The narcissist will end up focusing on others who are causing upset. The focus will never be on what the narcissist did wrong. It simply isn't possible, because the narcissist won't ever truly own problematic behaviors. There is always a caveat. The finger is forever pointed outward.

To better understand, it is important to consider how narcissists are formed. Typically, such a character defect is the result of a developmental arrest during a critical period of child development. It may have been due to abuse, neglect, excessive criticism from a parent, or a lack of love from a parent. Multiple paths can lead to that developmental arrest, including some kind of genetic predisposition, but think of it as a critical ingredient in the personality recipe that was left out or forgotten. The person continued to physically grow but did not develop a healthy ability to attach to others. This is sad, but it can never be remedied. You cannot love them into being a better person.

People who have a normal ability to attach to others spend countless hours trying to understand why the narcissist makes bad choices, why the narcissist doesn't show healthy love, and why the narcissist doesn't change. The answer is that the narcissist does not possess the ability to do these things because key ingredients for that recipe are missing.

The most important key ingredient that is missing is the ability to take a perspective beyond himself. A narcissist is unable to completely see other viewpoints or feel empathy, because he can't see beyond himself. Narcissists, therefore, lack the ability to engage in healthy love and attachment. Their hearts are not whole. Because healthy adults have a whole heart, they are not fully capable of understanding why narcissists don't. It all seems so confusing, but I assure you the exercise of trying to understand it will leave you with more frustration, no answers, and more confused. And the effort to try explaining your position is the psychological equivalent of beating your head against a wall. All that does is hurt your head; it doesn't affect the wall one bit.

The mindfuck is that narcissists are adept—for a while— at acting as if they have a heart. They have demonstrated moments that mimic love; but it isn't healthy love. There is no true heart. It is again part of the learned manipulation to get what he wants.

All of this significantly fucks with the head of the normally attaching adult. Add to that the high-level ability of the narcissist to blame the partner, and voila! The normally attaching adult feels like the breakup is her fault, there is something wrong with her, and she needs to get help so she can fix the relationship. She can be the person the narcissist would want. Even worse, the normally attaching person believes she needs to get help so she can help the narcissist stop behaving badly.

At this point, maybe you can see that narcissists are strongly attracted to people who are highly empathic and those with boundary issues. They want someone they can easily dump their bullshit on. They are also strongly attracted to people with codependency, because highly codependent people will also put up with extreme bullshit and try to fix it all like *they* are the one at fault.

This can be a toxic combination. The problem here arises when a normally attaching adult completely attaches to an adult who has no ability to attach. The normally attached adult has a very hard time letting go and walking away. That person cannot fathom that the other person can't be fixed. Recovery for the normally attached person often takes long as a result.

· **GETTING THERE** ·

Here are my recommendations for recovering from a breakup with a narcissist:

1. Recognize that a narcissist can never change, nor can they see themselves in truth. It's sad, but it's also a huge relief because you can let it go. It's not you, it's them . . . seriously. Don't take it personally.
2. Stop all contact as soon as possible. Narcissists want to be the center of attention. They feed on it. They have to have someone to give it to them. They need to feel important. At first, they

will forcefully try to insert themselves into your life—even if you try to push them out. This is what they do, especially by finding ways to fuck with your mind. They are looking for anything they can say or do to hook you back into interactions, including false apologies, lame excuses, or some reason to elicit your sympathy. Don't fall for it. Eventually, they will slither away. Starve their desire for attention by giving none. Even little sparks of attention feed the flame and drag out the misery. Resist answering that email, text, or phone call!

3. Surround yourself with friends, family, and supportive others. Form a layer of protection around yourself, and have a plan for when the narcissist tries to get a foot in the door. Ask these people to protect you if necessary—or, at least, be ready to remind you of the critical events you may have forgotten. In fact, keep a diary of the toxic, harmful things the narcissist has done. Have a list of activities to keep yourself busy when you feel vulnerable.

4. For the love of life, when you notice thoughts of the narcissist creeping in, catch these insidious self-talk thoughts:
    - This is my fault.
    - Maybe I misunderstood.
    - Maybe I didn't try hard enough.
    - Maybe he could get better with therapy.
    - We've had such good times. I hate to give up.
    - He's done so much for me/helped me when I needed it/ got me through a tough time or illness.

    Argue back. Call yourself out when you are telling the sad stories. Don't give the thoughts any oxygen, either. MOMF it up:
    - This is not how healthy love feels.
    - Motherfucker, you've hung in there for way too long. The math in this equation just isn't computing.

- Why do you think your friends and family all think he's such a dick? Honey, this ride's over.

The whole drive of the narcissist is to make everything about *him*. Don't you do that too. Don't let your thoughts become all about him. Don't allow thoughts of him to be a cancer in your mind.

5. Be kind to yourself. Exercise. Eat healthy. Do fun things. Spend time in nature. Allow yourself to heal. When you notice judgmental thoughts creeping in, tell them to fuck off. Don't do that to yourself. Treat yourself like you would a friend. Blame is the narcissist being present in your mind. When you blame yourself, it is him being present. No. No way. None of that. Have a sacred phrase to use every time a self-blaming thought arises, such as *fuck that*, *shut up*, or even a question like *is this really true?*

6. Journal, and journal more. Let out your feelings. Notice your growth. Pep yourself up. Eventually, write about the red flags you missed. Write about why you ignored your gut. Write about what you would do differently if you could go back in time . . . or the next time you meet someone like them. When you are ready, write a letter to your younger self. What advice would you give yourself? MOMF that up too (e.g., *Bitch, run like the wind when you see this one coming*). But be kind to yourself, too. (*Aw, honey, I know you want love so bad because you didn't get it when you were a kid, but you deserve so much better.*)

7. Write about the fairy tale you created in your mind compared to what you actually had. Be honest with yourself that what you made it into wasn't real. Write about the fairy tale where you said it could be salvaged when you knew it wasn't fixable. Perhaps you so wanted it to be real that you lied to yourself or ignored truths, but the narcissist doesn't have the

power to take away what you want in a truly loving relationship unless you give him that power.

8. Stop making everything about him. That is what he has brainwashed you into doing. You have to learn to stop doing that. Notice your thoughts and hold yourself accountable for spending time on them. You cannot control what thoughts pop into your mind. You can, however, control how much time you spend ruminating on them. Each time you do that, you are giving power and attention to the narcissist. This can stop any time you are ready. Yes, you are that powerful.

THE DEPENDENT

Camilla was a strong person. She knew what she wanted, and she made it happen. She met Marco at a friend's party. He wasn't the typical kind of guy she liked. He was pretty easygoing. He didn't have strong opinions, and he basically went with the flow of things. She was attracted to that. She got to call the shots. Plus, he listened to her. He took her seriously and highly valued her advice.

As they got more serious, Camilla started having doubts about Marco. If she told him to do something, he did it, but otherwise he didn't seem to have much drive. He liked to play video games— a lot. When she questioned why he wasn't more of a go-getter at work, he got neurotic and started whining. He expressed paralyzing self-doubt and asked her to tell him what to do. He began asking for her help more and more.

One day, Camilla realized their relationship had turned into a mother-son one. She had to admit that she had come to hate Marco, and she was even starting to dislike herself because she was being mean to him. She didn't know how to stop, and she didn't know how to leave. She worried that he would just fall apart without her—because, in fact, he'd told her many times that he would. She thought he was just being grateful. Now she could see that he believed it. She felt trapped and a little dirty.

Camilla was in a relationship with someone with dependency issues. People who are dependent are incredibly needy. It may be exhausting just to think about interacting with that person. In a relationship, it becomes as if the person cannot survive with you. At first, feeling important and useful had been a nice feeling, but it quickly became a prison.

People who are dependent are passive and have a hard time making decisions. It's as though they need someone to tell them what to do all the time. There is a clingy nature to the person; but rather than coming off as strong and controlling, it comes off as weak and pathetic. It is very easy to feel sorry for people who are dependent, because they appear fragile and vulnerable, like a child in the body of an adult. They are in need of constant reassurance.

The dependent person can't seem to figure out how to cope with or live life independently. They have high emotional needs—needing comfort, advice, support. It is exhausting to be around.

At some point, cleaning up the messes and figuring out what to do next feels more like parenting than partnering. People in a relationship with a dependent often feel a strong mix of anger, resentment, frustration, guilt, and sadness. They very much want to leave the person but feel like they'd be abandoning the family pet without any way to survive on its own. Nice, right? I have to tell you, this isn't an adult relationship if you feel that way about your partner.

As with narcissism, the root of dependence likely goes back to childhood and a genetic predisposition. People who are highly dependent never learned independent living skills as a child and may have had one or two caregivers who did too much, but it isn't about being spoiled. Dependency is about the core belief *I can't do it by myself.* The issue is not just wanting someone to fix and help; it is about needing the help and not being able to function without it. The underlying issue is with a core sense of self.

While I feel a little more hopeful that dependence can be improved somewhat with intensive therapy, there are many caveats. First, the dependent person must be fully invested in learning to be independent. They also have to have a deep capacity to self-reflect and tolerate the painful emotions associated with examining how they are perceived by others. As you might imagine, this takes courage, strength, and stamina. It also takes time. Treatment would likely take years of solid investment to see fruitful change.

Second, the end outcome would *not* be that the person is no longer dependent. Instead, the person would be *less* dependent. Third and perhaps most important, anyone in a relationship with a dependent person would have to determine if the relationship dynamics *could* change. People who are dependent are drawn to people who like to control (or vice versa). In order for a dependent person to improve, it would be important to be away from others who are constantly trying to save the day, control and fix. Furthermore, the partner would need to determine if he is able to get over the anger, frustration, and resentment of the dependent person and if he wants to take the risk of putting life on hold. It may be that change could never happen if the two people stay together anyway. The dynamic of giver and taker is just too strong. If a person does decide to stick it out, I think understanding *why* would be incredibly important.

· **GETTING THERE** ·

My recommendations for recovering from a breakup with a dependent are:

1. Use the Getting There suggestions from the section on the narcissist.
2. Cut off contact. Continued contact will only lead to more sadness, more guilt, and more anguish. It will not be helpful for either of you to continue feeding off of one another. It will be sad to cut off contact because you will worry, but true change cannot happen while you are there to save the day. Leaving is actually an act of kindness because you will stop enabling. The sadness will get better.
3. Get into therapy and more deeply understand why you put up with so much bullshit. What needs are you trying to fill in the wrong ways? How can you better handle your desire to control and fix? What red flags did you miss? What do you to need to do to make sure this doesn't happen again?
4. Journal your thoughts and feelings. Resist the urge to reach out. You ex can't begin to heal until you leave them alone.

THE SOCIOPATH

Ashti and Noah met at work. He was incredibly charming and worked as an IT consultant for Ashti's firm. He helped her solve a complex work dilemma and they agreed to go for a drink afterward. The rest is history.

Noah swept Ashti off of her feet. What she most admired about him was that he could talk his way into anything. They got upgrades, cuts in line, and all kinds of special perks when they went out.

Over time she noticed he was comfortable breaking the rules more so than she. Occasionally, he would let something slip about how he conned someone at work or took advantage of a situation. Ashti frowned upon this, but she told herself it was because Noah was so creative. I mean, he wasn't a bad guy. He couldn't be.

She also began to catch him in lies. Sometimes he would spend excessive time explaining why she had misunderstood, and other times, he would tell her that she just didn't understand why he had to lie. He sometimes convinced her that she made things up or misunderstood/misheard. Noah was like nonstick cookware . . . nothing would stick.

One day, she discovered he had electronically spied on a co-worker. She was appalled. This led to more distrust in their relationship, and Ashti decided to end it even though she still loved Noah.

Noah didn't take it well. Strange things started happening to her. Her identity was stolen, and her computer was hacked. She began to think she was being watched and monitored. She notified the police and was fearful for her safety. She always had the feeling that he was in the shadows. He told lies about her at work that caused some problems with her boss. The police contacted her stating Noah had even filed a complaint against her for harassment. She had to go down to the station and call an attorney. Ashti worried it would never end. Part of her knew Noah was capable of hurting her, but another part of her didn't want to accept that he would.

This is scary. Sociopaths lack a conscience and empathy. They are out for *numero uno*. Silly things like laws, rules, and social norms are merely suggestions—not meant for them. Sociopaths will go to great lengths to get what they want, even if it means destroying others.

They have no guilt or remorse.

This is all very hard for the normal person to understand. The normal person feels guilt, remorse, and empathy. We cannot imagine being unable to feel these things, so we deny that the person we are involved with is that sort of person. What would that say about us? Admitting we are or were connected with a sociopath also means admitting something about ourselves. We may have to admit that we have denied facts, or at least been blind to them. We may have been overly tolerant of bad behavior or made excuses for it. It isn't pretty to acknowledge that we played a role in being in such a bad place.

The sociopath is very similar to the narcissist. In fact, you may wish to think about the sociopath being narcissistic *and* amoral. Again, going back to childhood, sociopaths did not develop the ability to attach *or* care for others. The sociopath never developed a sense of right or wrong. Sociopaths are not able to take the perspective of another person. They have no empathy. Sociopaths can only see things through their own eyes. The confusing part, however, is that they can skillfully pretend to care for others and to see others' perspectives. They are masters of the con arts. They are experts at playing on others' emotions. It's paradoxical how well sociopaths do at using another person's emotions against him without understanding at all how he feels.

Sociopaths are capable of all kinds of damage and destruction in other people's lives, particularly because nothing is off limits as long as they want it. The worst kind of damage, though, is the emotional damage they are able to inflict on others. Sociopaths tend to be charming—and, again, they are well able to con others emotionally. Therefore, they often easily insinuate themselves into the lives of unwitting and trusting people whose lives they'll leave in shambles without a speck of remorse.

There is no fix for sociopaths. As with the narcissist, the damage goes back to childhood and is often related to early-life abuse and neglect. The damage is, sadly, irreversible. Therapy is not only *not* useful; it is contraindicated, because the sociopaths are not capable of being honest in therapy. It is a waste of time. There is no need for beating oneself up for getting involved with a sociopath. Everyone is vulnerable. You are only guilty of a kind heart and trusting soul. And maybe of not listening to your gut.

· GETTING THERE ·

Here are my recommendations for recovering from a breakup with a sociopath:

1. Use the Getting There suggestions from the section on the narcissist.
2. Protect yourself. It is better to plan for the worst than to be unprepared. Until you are assured the person is out of your life, don't let your guard down. Maybe you stay with friends. Maybe you have extra security, both physical and electronic. Consider an order of personal protection through the police department. Just be sure that you are protecting yourself.
3. Cut off contact. Do not delude yourself into thinking you can placate or outfox a sociopath. Remember, this is their specialty. You cannot outplay a player. Don't give money. Don't fall into blackmail. Sociopaths like to use fear as a primary motivator. If you give in to that, you will create a pattern. The best thing you can do is ignore, ignore, ignore. That includes attacks of most kinds (other than physical). Resist reacting or retaliating! That's what they want.
4. Just be smart. Do not let your emotions guide your decisions. Use your head. Surround yourself with good friends who will speak truth to you and help you make good decisions.
5. Tell yourself it will get better. And it will, as long as you keep your distance. Eventually, the sociopath will move on to someone else. Don't ever look back.

THE ABUSER

Years ago, when I was an undergrad, I found a cute little apartment for my senior year. It was a hidden gem directly above my landlady's living quarters. It was clean, safe, and obviously cared-for. I felt so lucky.

During this time, I was a volunteer at the county domestic violence shelter. My main duty was to take crisis calls on the domestic-violence hotline, which were routed to my home phone. The job entailed answering phone calls mostly from women who were in abusive relationships. Sometimes they just wanted to talk. Sometimes they wanted to know what resources were available. Sometimes they wanted help escaping. It was great, because I could do this work from the safety of my couch.

The one thing that was drilled into me as a volunteer was that leaving an abusive relationship is the most dangerous time in the cycle of abuse. It is not appropriate to just tell someone to leave, because it isn't that cut-and-dried. As this is when the person who wants to leave is most likely to be killed, it's not a risk to be taken lightly.

There are very real safety issues. Planning for contingencies and gathering money, important papers, and essential belongings are important. These things need time and consideration if possible. Sometimes people don't leave abusive relationships, because it feels safer to stay than to risk being killed. That is an incredibly tormenting dilemma, especially when kids are involved.

Anyway, it is extraordinarily ironic that while I was taking these phone calls, I was terrified for my own safety. You see, my landlady had a live-in boyfriend who was built like a brick shithouse. I could hear them fighting all the time. It was bad, very bad, because mostly I could only hear him yelling, and it sounded violent. I would often become paralyzed with fear that he was going to kill her, and then he would have to come and kill me too because I would be a witness.

When I would see her out and about, she always wore a shit ton of makeup—likely to cover bruises. She was about five feet tall and slight. So many times I wanted to say to her that I could help, though I wasn't sure how to say it. I never said anything.

I didn't know what to do. Should I help? Call the police? Do something? or nothing? I was petrified. I didn't want to make it worse. I didn't want him to come after me. I didn't want to be evicted. This was only a small insight into the fear and paralysis experienced by a person being abused. I can only imagine what it must be like.

Given this experience, I want to say first and foremost that I don't take leaving an abusive situation lightly. If possible, it should be thought out, planned, and methodical in order to increase safety. I recognize, though, it cannot always be that way. Sometimes you just get the hell out when you can and deal with the rest later. There is no one-size-fits-all.

I want you to know that you are not alone. There are many, many people who care, even if you don't know them yet. Above all else, I want you to know that no one deserves to be abused. It doesn't matter what you have done in the past. It doesn't matter what decisions you made that contributed to the situation. It doesn't matter about your looks, your education, your upbringing, or your mistakes. There is no excuse for anyone violently laying hands on another person, other than in self-defense.

Many people are brainwashed into believing something they said or did caused the abuse. Unless you have some kind of mind or behavioral control over someone else (hint: this is not possible), you cannot be responsible for another person's choices. Abuse and violence are choices. Let me say this again: abuse and violence are choices that someone else made. While you may tell yourself that your partner *can't help it*, let me assure you that he *can* help it; he just doesn't want to.

It is the brainwashing and realistic fear of increasing the violence that traps people in abusive relationships. It is guilt that past decisions led to this. It is a feeling that one doesn't deserve better. It is also a fear that things will be worse elsewhere. At least within an abusive relationship, there is some predictability. You will have food and shelter. That is more than a person may be guaranteed elsewhere.

All of this explains why people stay.

I want you to also clearly hear me say that there is hope, and there are options. Leaving will not be easy, and there will be no silver bullet. But change cannot occur until you decide to create it. I am suggesting, though, that—unlike other relationships—leaving should be thoughtful.

· GETTING THERE ·

Here are my recommendations for leaving an abuser:

1. Use the Getting There suggestions from the section on the narcissist.
2. I encourage you to put your safety above all else. It doesn't matter if it is overkill. Better to be safe than sorry. I also implore you to consult your local domestic-violence hotline. The national number is 800-799-7233, or you can text LOVEIS to 22522. The website is thehotline.org. Because these folks are the experts, they have thought of things you haven't. They have helpful guidance, and they have resources—even free legal help. There is also counseling and group therapy for adults and children. You can talk

with others who have been where you are and emerged in one piece. It helps. Domestic-violence shelters provide food, clothes, and shelter. Their locations are secret so abusers cannot find you, and they have security. You aren't alone there. Domestic violence programs also understand what you are experiencing. I am confident they've heard it all. They are on your side and want to help you without judgment.

3. While there is a valid reason for you to be afraid, you cannot let fear stop you from envisioning a different life. Fear should inform you so you make good decisions, but fear should not paralyze you or stop you. That is the brainwashing. That is the control. You have the ability to transcend. Perhaps you need to rediscover that, but it is present within you. I strongly recommend counseling to process the trauma you have experienced, to make sense of it, and to learn to manage its aftermath. There is a way out. Sometimes you need someone to shine the light for you to see the way. Again, you are not alone.

4. I cannot promise you a smooth road. I cannot guarantee a fairy-tale ending. I can only tell you that you are worth considering something better. You are worth kindness, respect, and a safe place to live, regardless of any previous choices you have made. You are worthy.

THE THREATENER

Daniel had been dating Marc for nine months. Most of that time had been really good, but they were just very different people. Daniel had been going to counseling and figured out that Marc just wasn't the one for him. He spent time in counseling, troubleshooting the best way to break the news to Marc. Daniel was a nice guy and felt that Marc deserved to be told the truth in person.

One night he suggested they get together for dinner, and he just told Marc it was over. Marc was devastated and started crying. He said he didn't want to live without Daniel. He went on and on about how important he was to him, and how he'd become a better person with him. Marc pointed out that he had been on anti-depressants before they met, but he no longer needed them with Daniel. Because Daniel had been coached well by a therapist, he stuck to his guns and ended the relationship. He felt like shit, but it needed to be done.

Marc started texting Daniel that he was going to kill himself. His life was not worth living, and he had nothing to live for. He began berating himself. At first, Daniel engaged with Marc, trying to talk him down. He even agreed to go over to his house and soothe him. This resulted in Marc trying to come on to Daniel in an attempt to repair the relationship. Daniel didn't give in, but he also was having second thoughts.

He felt incredible pressure because Marc's dad had died when he was younger, and he had a lot of conflict with his mother. Marc was an only child and didn't have a lot of friends. Daniel felt like Marc relied on him solely for emotional support, and now he wasn't there. Daniel had a hard time tolerating the idea that he would be responsible for Marc hurting himself. When Marc saw Daniel, he told him his life was in Daniel's hands.

Daniel vacillated between being pissed and feeling trapped. He discussed it with his therapist in an effort to find the right solution. It was a moral decision, right? He had to make the right choice so that Marc was safe . . . or so he thought.

While I have seen all of the previously mentioned bad actors threaten themselves with harm in order to control the person who is leaving, the threatener is also a category of its own. This category is about extreme emotional manipulation, and I want to give it special attention because it is so, so common.

The threatener is the person who threatens "bad things will

happen to me if you leave." Notably, the threatener often says "If you leave, I will kill myself." Or "I can't live without you. I'd rather die." I have seen this time and time again, and it is incredibly disturbing for the person who wants to leave.

As most loving people do, the person who wants to leave feels trapped. He feels like he can't do what he needs and wants to do for his own well-being because the other person may die. That's a lot of responsibility to process. It is one thing to know that you are hurting another person; but it is a whole different ball game being told that the other person will die if you leave.

The person who wants to leave now feels responsible for the threatener's safety—their life or death. This tactic can be highly effective for the threatener in his effort to hold on to the partner, but it is blackmail. It is extortion. It's bullshit.

Why does the threatener do this? Clearly, it is emotional manipulation meant to fuck with their erstwhile partner's mind and keep her around. I want to call out right now how unfair it is to ever put responsibility for one's choices on someone else. This is the ultimate cop-out. It is inappropriate. It is fucked up. It wrong to the core. If you give in to this, you will be reinforcing the method as effective.

Do not be held hostage to emotional terrorism. If someone chooses to hurt himself, that is *that* person's choice. Remember you do not have the special power of mind control, you do not control another person's choices.

All that being said, I have been talking about true bad actors who use threats as a means of controlling someone else. At the same time, there may be legitimate cases of depression or other mental illness that cause someone to consider suicide during a time of loss. Because it isn't your job to figure out what is emotional manipulation and what is a genuine threat, call 911. Call 911 every single time the person threatens. The emergency authorities are tasked with treating people who need emergency care.

This is the most kind, compassionate thing you can do for someone, because if that person is truly suicidal, you can't fix it just by sticking around. Professional help is needed. Your job is done.

· GETTING THERE ·

Here is what I recommend when breaking up with the threatener:

1. Use the Getting There suggestions from the section on the narcissist.

2. Each and every one of us has to be responsible for our own choices. When someone threatens to kill himself, he is using the most extreme form of emotional manipulation. It is like holding another person emotionally hostage. Ending a relationship does not cause suicide. Suicide is a choice, and it cannot be blamed on someone else. Relationships end all the time, and the vast majority of folks don't kill themselves. In fact, even those who threaten to do so often don't kill themselves. If anything, a threatener may make a gesture to hurt himself to garner more attention. In that circumstance, the threatener may hurt himself unintentionally. How fucked up is that? This isn't a game. Ending a relationship does not cause suicide. You are not responsible. You take care of yourself.

3. End contact with the threatener. You clearly cannot have healthy conversations. Continued conversations are painful for both of you. No one can move on. Also, do not continue conversations with the threatener's mother, siblings, or extended family. They understandably want to include you because they want to help their loved one (they see you as the solution to the possible demise of the threatener); but again, this is not healthy for you. It is not okay to put someone else's

wants above your own. Notice I didn't say someone else's "needs." What they *need* is professional help. You cannot give this, so there is no point in trying. We are talking about someone else's *wants,* and your job is to focus on your own wants and needs.

4. I wish I could tell you that if you do these things, you won't feel like shit. Unfortunately, you probably will, but it will get better without contact. Remind yourself this is not healthy. It is not normal, and it isn't something you can fix.

RISK REDUCTION

Wow, this chapter was full of some heavy stuff. I so wish I could give you a foolproof formula for avoiding people with these traits—but if one exists, I don't have it. At the same time, I can assure you that by doing one thing and one thing alone, you can decrease your risk of relationships with people like this and with messed-up people in general.

Wait for it . . . here it is:

Lower your bullshit tolerance. You heard me. At the first whiff of bullshit, walk away. It may save you in the end. The kinds of folks I detail in this chapter are drawn to people who are super-nice. They are drawn to people who put up with too much bullshit. (Check out chapter 8 for a lot more on this.) Why? Because they won't get far with people who walk away. Consider being a little less nice to stray people. Be a little more selective about people with sketchy life histories or who regale you with the drama in their current and past life. Maybe raise your standards to what you deserve.

I'm not saying to be an asshole. That isn't the solution. Life isn't that black-and-white anyway. There are more choices than being a kind, compassionate savior to all or being an asshole. It is about finding a common ground. Certain bullshit is unnecessary. Stop treating it all as though it is required.

That isn't to say that if you do all of the things I suggest, you will completely avoid these extra-special types of assholes, because we are all vulnerable. No one is immune to getting taken. I'm just saying that the higher your standards, the more riffraff you leave behind.

Good luck out there. It's a jungle.

8

Boundaries: The Bullshit Stops Here

Warning: This chapter can be emotionally heavy.

I know. I know. All of the chapters in this book are emotionally heavy. I take no pleasure in the possibility that this one may be more so than the others.

While the topic of boundaries may seem straightforward, it cuts so much deeper. Boundaries go to the heart of the emotional learning we experienced as children. The insights you have from this chapter may hurt a bit more than other chapters, because I am switching the focus from your ex to you.

You may want to take it more slowly and really let it sink in.

MALIK AND CHLOE

Malik and Chloe had lived together for seven years. When they'd first started dating, they were in their late twenties. Life was all about fun. They partied a fair amount, but they both had a good time. No one got hurt. Over time, Malik wanted to lay off partying so much. He needed to focus at work, and feeling like shit the next day made it too hard. Plus, it was not fun anymore. Chloe, on the other hand, was all about drinking, getting high, and socializing. This caused increasing conflict as she labeled Malik "a downer," and he labeled her "out of control."

They fought more and more, and Malik found himself looking up substance-abuse programs for her. He would present his findings to her, but she would laugh and tell him to stop acting like an old man. He talked with Chloe's sister, and they would conspire about how to intervene. He found himself spending more and more time cleaning up Chloe's messes, covering for her when she didn't follow through on responsibilities, and fighting with her about changing her ways.

Malik was angry, but he was also not yet ready to be done with the relationship. He had grown up in a single-parent home. As the oldest child in his family, he'd learned a strong sense of responsibility in taking care of his younger brothers and sisters when his mom wasn't around, which was a lot.

He shared his frustrations with a buddy, who told him to get the fuck out now; but Malik feared she would get even worse if he left. He also knew she didn't have the money to survive on her own. Malik told himself Chloe would eventually to see the light. She just needed his help.

LEARNING BOUNDARIES

There is no bigger issue in relationships than boundaries. Think of boundaries as limits that demarcate where something ends and something else begins. Boundaries are important so you can know what is what, where is what, and whose is what.

We learn about boundaries early in life. Think about it. Two-year-olds have two favorite words: "No" and "Mine." These are both boundary words. These words let others know where we stand, how we feel, what we will put up with, and when to back off.

If others around us respected our boundary pronouncements as kids, we learned how to stand up for ourselves—not just as two-year-olds, but throughout childhood. You know, "don't touch my shit"; "no means no"; "get out of my room."

When I say "respect boundary pronouncements," I don't mean that people just did what we demanded. That isn't realistic. Boundaries are not selfish demands that we put on others. Boundaries are statements or understandings about preferences and tolerance limits and what is okay and what is not okay.

While I cannot expect that boundary preferences will always be honored by others (for example, I may have a boundary around being with annoying people, but I can't expect that annoying people will just go away), I am saying that our spoken preferences (like I prefer not to be touched) should be treated respectfully. [To be clear here, I am not talking about a two-year-old who doesn't want to be held back from doing something dangerous or who doesn't want a bath. I am talking about a person who is old enough to communicate a desire to not be touched when touch is not necessary.] If the stated boundary cannot be honored, there should be an explanation as to why, so we can decide what to do next. This is much different than having boundaries forcefully violated or having our wishes ignored. Boundaries for kids are formed by the way parents and important adults respond when the kids assert themselves.

Boundaries are also affected by inappropriate invasions of privacy. (I say "inappropriate" because parents do need to be all up in their kids' shit. Monitoring online activity is an example of appropriate invasions of privacy. Inappropriate invasions of privacy refer to *accidentally* walking in on a kid getting dressed in private.) Boundaries are influenced by caregivers who model how to say "no" when needed and how to stop others from being invasive.

In relationships, boundaries are about deciding and communicating to others what shit is yours and what shit is not yours, and who is responsible for what shit. Boundaries are relevant to all kinds of relationships and settings (romantic, work, friendships, family, social).

Growing up, if you were surrounded by people who got dumped on or you experienced others dumping their shit on you, you may have learned to feel responsible for others' shit. If people invaded your privacy on a regular basis, you may have learned that boundaries are fluid and not firm. You may have learned that it is hard to say "no" and be accepted or respected.

In a more stark and violent way, if you experienced someone touching your body inappropriately, you may have learned that there are no boundaries. Think about it for a minute. If, as a child, you learned that people could just touch your body as they wanted, even when you expressed discomfort, what control over limits would you learn? It's really quite basic.

STAGES OF PSYCHOSOCIAL DEVELOPMENT

It can be helpful to consider Erik Erikson's classic and timeless model of human development, the Stages of Psychosocial Development.[19] When people tell me about their struggles, I often reflect on Erikson's model to help me better understand how past events affected development and current struggles. I am going to summarize the early life stages below, and I want you to consider how childhood experiences could affect boundary development.

- **Basic Trust vs. Mistrust (Birth–18 months old):** During this stage, a child learns trust if her needs are consistently met by caregivers, if she is cared for with love. Mistrust is learned if needs are not met or if life and those in it are unpredictable.

- **Autonomy vs. Shame (1–3 years old):** During this stage, a child is experimenting with newly found freedoms. He can learn a sense of independence by being given the freedom to try new things, or he can learn fear, shame, and doubt if he is punished for independence or discouraged from it.

- **Initiative vs. Guilt (3–5 years old):** In many ways, this stage is a continuation of the previous one. It is gaining more independence and confidence in decision-making. This stage is about a child learning to take initiative in doing new things, making new friends, and experimenting. If the child is encouraged to do this safely, she develops a sense of self-confidence. If a child is discouraged, held back, or prevented from independence, a sense of guilt can result.

- **Industry vs. Inferiority (6–11 years old):** Much more social comparison happens in this stage. Kids begin to look at peers and evaluations from teachers and parents for evidence of competency and adequacy. If kids do not receive validation of their worth and adequacy, they can develop self-doubt and self-esteem struggles.

- **Identity vs. Role Confusion (12–18 years old):** The major question of this stage is: Who am I? Kids also are struggling with questions of: What is my place in the world? Where am I going? There is a lot going on at this stage. Kids are experimenting with a lot of ideas. They may be argumentative and not even know why. They are working to form personal beliefs, ideals, values, and goals. This stage is crucial to forming identity. Kids need room to try out new ideas without judgment (safely, of course). If adults do not respect kids' autonomy by giving them enough space to sort it out, kids can develop identity confusion and a disrupted sense of self.

There are more stages, but I am focused here on early development. Consider how being disrespected or not honored consistently at each stage may affect boundary development.

If you are a parent, do *not* take a side journey into parent guilt here. Parents have a super-hard job, and it is not about respecting *all* of your children's wishes and boundaries. That would create a monster. What I am talking about here is consistent boundary violations that undercut a child's independence. I am talking about abusive types of boundary violations.

· GETTING THERE ·

Think back to your childhood. Can you identify any flashbulb moments that stand out regarding boundaries? Draw a timeline, and note these significant moments in your life on the timeline. Note how old you were and what Erikson stage you were at. How do you think these experiences affected your sense of boundaries? When you think of your core beliefs, how did these experiences inform how you see yourself, others, and the world? How do these core beliefs affect your self-talk and relationships?

WHY BOUNDARIES ARE IMPORTANT

If you think back to what I've said previously about personality and core belief development, you know that the emotional learning around boundaries is persistent. This means that even if you read, understand, and agree with everything I am saying about healthy boundaries, you may continue to feel guilty, bad, and ashamed even when you set boundaries. That is because you cannot go back and re-learn emotional lessons. All you can do is recognize that you learned some unhealthy things at critical junctures in your life. You can acknowledge that the emotional reaction isn't rational: it is an artifact of the past.

Just because you feel the emotion does not mean the emotion is fact-based. Setting boundaries may be the most painful experience a person can have if that person did not learn to do it early in life. It feels bad and wrong, but it is *not* bad and wrong. When sorting it out, it is important to stay in your head with the facts.

Boundaries are important because they hold you together. It can be overwhelming to live life and feel responsible for others' feelings, reactions, and other bullshit. Seriously, your own bullshit is enough.

CODEPENDENCE

People who struggle with boundaries almost always struggle with codependence. Codependence is the tendency to overfunction in relationships. This enables other people to continue dysfunctional behavior. Codependence is about doing too much for others, out of a drive or misguided desire to help.

I know that codependence has a negative connotation, but I think of it as something all humans run the risk of doing. I like to think most humans have some desire to help. Some people want to help a lot and others very little. When the desire to help is too strong, it can turn into codependence, particularly among those who struggle with boundaries—either recognizing boundaries or holding them.

A person who is strong on codependence has a hard time knowing when and how to say no and has a hard time determining who is responsible for the problem at the time.

Here's the thing: people who like to help and fix are drawn

to—or attract—people who want to use, consume, or rely on others to fix their problems. In other words, givers attract takers, and vice versa.

What's odd is that people who are high on codependence often complain that they hate the pressure and burden associated with everyone else's problems. If that is the case, why does it keep happening? It goes back to childhood stuff. Fixers never learned to say no and were not given permission to say no. In fact, it may have been quite the opposite: fixers may have been emotionally brainwashed through guilt and punishment to avoid saying no. Fixing is familiar, even if isn't always pleasant. It fills a need or drive to help, and the person is often unaware that stopping is actually an option.

People who are drawn to fixing others' problems often find themselves with people who have a lot of problems. It can be easy to fall into the rabbit hole of feeling like you need to—or have to—help. You tell yourself terrible, heartbreaking stories of what might happen if you don't help. It can feel like you have no choice.

There are also people who are drawn to fixing because it makes them feel good, helpful, or powerful. Fixing can give a false sense of control or power in an otherwise chaotic life.

The part that may be the most painful is knowing that you should stop trying to fix and step back, but feeling like doing so would willingly hurt someone else or worse, ruining others' lives. That storyline is there. It is scary as hell, and it won't go away. Yet it is flawed.

You can see how horribly difficult it would be to resist this storyline. Clearly, it is faulty and distorted, but it is the only one the person living the storyline knows. They often have no idea that there is any other way to live, because it's all they've known. Perhaps no one has told the person that attention to self and self-care are healthy and good. Likely, they were taught that it's selfish.

· GETTING THERE: CODEPENDENCE ASSESSMENT ·

I've come up with some questions to help you better assess your level of codependence. These questions aren't meant to be scored, but rather are aimed to help you better understand yourself and what you bring to the table.

1. How much time do I spend on other people's problems, compared to my own happiness?
2. How much do I beat myself up for not doing more to help others?
3. How much responsibility do I take for helping others fix problems that are not directly mine?
4. How much guilt do I feel when I can't or don't help others?
5. How important do I feel when I help others?
6. How hard is it for me to stand up for myself and speak my mind?
7. How hard is it for me to say no when others ask me to do something?
8. How hard is it for me to spend time on myself?
9. How preoccupied am I with the thought of making someone upset?
10. How much time do I spend apologizing for not doing more?
11. How much of my own happiness do I give up for others?
12. How important is it for me to have others' approval?

The more you found yourself answering "a lot," the more codependence you struggle with. The actual number isn't important, as far as I am concerned. It isn't as though the goal is to get you to zero, because then you'd be an asshole.

The goal of this exercise is to help you self-reflect, raise your own consciousness, and examine your boundaries.

To review, people who are high on codependence have such a skewed idea of helping others that any time spent on themselves feels selfish. They feel like they can't say no. They worry about upsetting others and spend way too much time apologizing and pleasing. A primary motivating feeling in life is guilt. That is not okay.

What stands out to you as you reflect on your answers? Identify one or two areas where you would like to practice setting some boundaries. Set some goals. Write about these in your journal.

BACK TO RELATIONSHIPS

In the previous chapter, we looked at special circumstances in the other person that make breakups complicated and super-messy. This chapter relates to complications within *you* that can make breakups complicated and super-messy.

If you are high on codependence, be aware that your ex assuredly knows that and will use it against you. My money is on the idea that if you are high on codependence, the other person has already manipulated you with guilt to get what she wanted. I could be wrong, but it would not be unusual.

People who struggle with high codependence and boundary issues take on way too much blame when things go awry in relationships, especially if the other person is blaming. The codependent person is often too willing to take on responsibility and blame—sometimes all of it. It's second nature. The codependent person excessively ruminates about what she could have done differently and what she did wrong along the way. The result is a one-sided blame shitstorm for all the things that went wrong.

This all assumes that a breakup even occurs. More often in a relationship, a person who is codependent is like gold to a user. There is no desire on the user's part to break up. The person with high codependence may be incredibly unhappy but never feel able to leave, because of the storyline that makes leaving the ultimate act of selfish betrayal. The storyline is that the other person needs the fixer. No matter how badly things go or how badly one is treated, the fixer stays. Even if a breakup occurs, the fixer may try to go back because of the storyline.

I may have made it sound just a little one-sided. Fixers do also get something else out of fixing. It fuels a drive to feel important. If you consider it, how good does it feel deeper down to know that someone *needs* you to problem-solve—to survive? This is something that also needs examination in order to move past a breakup. Remember core beliefs? It isn't that the drive to feel important goes away; it's learning that it is there and how to manage it.

· GETTING THERE ·

In summary, boundaries and codependence issues make breakups really hard. The struggle happens because giving up feels sad, wrong, and scary. It is also because there may be a restlessness about what to do with newfound time and energy. The sense of no longer being needed by someone else can leave a strong sense of emptiness. As I have said over and over, it is important to know who you are and what drives you so you can be on top of your own bullshit. You *can* be smarter than yourself. You can get ahead.

When you put together the knowledge of significant events from your childhood with data from the self-assessment on codependence, how does this information help you understand your drives and motivations? Logistically, what do you need to do to fill the emptiness left when you stop trying to fix others? How can you redirect the energy behind those drives into something healthier and more productive in your life?

By this point in the book, you have had time to try some of the suggested strategies to manage negative self-talk. When you consider boundaries and codependence, what negative self-talk will trip you up, and what strategies will work for you to manage the terrible, scary stories you tell yourself?

RECOMMENDED READING

Beattie, Melody. *Codependent No More*. Center City, MN: Hazelden Foundation, 1992.

9

Addicted to Love

Megan and Jimbo had a magnetic attraction. Sex was beyond amazing. Megan said she felt so alive when she was with him. He was so much fun. They had many common interests, and being together was just so effortless. Plus, there was intense passion between them. Jimbo confessed to her that he'd had a shitty childhood, with an absent dad and a mom who brought home a parade of questionable men. He told her that this caused him to have commitment issues, but he felt she could make him a changed man. Hearing this caused Megan to feel even closer with him. He'd let her into his innermost feelings. The connection was unreal.

Megan had had a pretty good childhood, even though her dad was "an alcoholic." He functioned okay with her mom's help. That's what love is about, anyway. You help one another.

She was thrilled to find a guy who appreciated her, and he lavished her with compliments. Over time, Megan could see a dark side to Jimbo. When he was up, things were better than ever. When he was down, however, everything was bad. He didn't drink every day like her dad, but he tied one on every so often. Those times were ugly, but Megan felt good that she could help Jimbo with his demons where other women had failed.

He'd started to become more flirtatious with other women in front of her, and she caught him kissing another girl at a party. They'd fought about this, but Jimbo had begged forgiveness, insisting that this was part of his baggage. He needed her to help him. Plus, he blamed her for pushing him to the infidelity, because she didn't believe in him. Maybe she could dress sexier next time.

This pissed Megan off, but then they had incredible sex that night. Things went back to baseline, and she vowed to work harder to help him with his past demons. He was opening up more to her and sharing how certain things about her troubled him—like her friendliness to others, her success at work, how easy she had it in life. He wanted to be more like her, and he kind of resented her for being so wonderful. He asked Megan for time and patience.

She began to catch Jimbo in multiple lies. She saw flirtatious behavior on social media that crossed lines. Her friends told her to cut bait and run. She could see their worry as valid, but she also knew they didn't know the Jimbo that she did. She was angry about his behavior, but she wasn't ready to quit on him yet. He had so much potential. She decided he just needed counseling, although the last time she'd brought this up he'd exploded that he wasn't "some head case."

The blowups and lies continued. Megan hated it. She hated herself for engaging in it, yet she hated the thought of leaving even more. The good times were just too damned good, even if they were few and far between. She was hooked on the intense highs.

I CAN'T STOP MYSELF

It is common for people to talk rationally with me about how toxic their ex is. They can list a litany of reprehensible qualities.

They are perfectly agreeable with the observation that they are better off without the ex and should stay away. They tell me they are struggling because they still love the ex, and I get it. You can't shut off love like it's a switch. I tell them that even though we feel the feelings of attachment, we may know we shouldn't act on them.

Then, these people say to me "But I can't stop. I can't stay away."

Whoa, Nellie! This is where we part ways. "Can't" means that you don't have the ability to do something. Since I know people have the ability to stop engaging with another human, I know the issue isn't ability. Perhaps it is *belief* in ability, but that's another story.

These same people often ask me if I think they are addicted to toxic people. According to Dictionary.com,[16] addiction is "the state of being enslaved to a habit or practice or to something that is psychologically or physically habit-forming, as narcotics, to such an extent that its cessation causes severe trauma."

For those professionals who treat addiction, they are talking about substances a person feels compelled to use despite all of the negative consequences. There is a component of physical and psychological craving that can cause people to lie and cheat to get what they want, and it can take over a person's life. The drive to use exists despite knowledge of terrible consequences.

I get how people compare going back (over and over) to a toxic relationship, which is destroying their lives in a way similar to substance-abuse addiction. And if I could hook folks up to functional brain imaging, I'm guessing I would see the *high* when they reunite with a toxic person in the same part of the brain as a person using drugs.

Honestly, I don't concern myself much with whether or not to call toxic relationships like that an addiction: I am more concerned with what to do about it. My biggest concern is when people start to think of an ex as an addiction that they *can't* resist, as if they are giving themselves permission to give up. I can't get distracted with the issue of whether or not we are going to call it an addiction—because in the end, the larger point is how to stop it, whatever you call it.

Fuck *can't*. That is giving up. Let's talk a bit about *can*.

LET'S CALL IT ADDICTION

If you are married to the idea of comparing toxic relationships to addiction, then let's go with it. I believe addiction is a disease that some people are more prone to because of genetics or traumatic life experiences. The high can be many things—substances, porn, experiences, and, yeah, maybe the experience of being connected to another person. The genetics and life-history parts are set and cannot be changed.

If you were born with anxious or high-strung traits and you experienced trauma or abuse as a child, or had parents who behaved in fucked-up ways, perhaps this increased your risk of being drawn to and tolerating toxic relationships. Perhaps part of your brain lights up when relationships become intense. Perhaps part of your brain lights up when you fight, because you feel alive in making up afterward. Perhaps this is all you know.

How's that working for you? How has acting on your impulses destroyed parts of your life? How have you allowed your feelings and desires to control well-thought-out choices?

All addiction requires treatment, but part of treatment is recognizing that you are who you are. You can get pissed about it. You can rail about how unfair it is. But in the end, you have what you have. The question is, what will you do with it?

Addiction as a disease is treatable. Just because someone has an addiction doesn't mean that the person is then fucked for life. I don't say "Oh, well, you are addicted. Sucks to be you."

Whether or not someone has an addiction to a toxic ex, just doesn't know how to leave, or doesn't feel strong enough to leave, "can't" isn't in the equation. It is a choice. I am not saying it is an easy choice, but staying or going is a choice. You may not like the choices. Fair. You may feel like one is too difficult. Fair. Let's get this straight, though. It isn't about ability.

It is about changing behavior.

I HAVE A PROBLEM

Fortunately, there is a lot that we know about how to treat addiction. It starts with identifying where you are in the process of change. James Prochaska, Ph.D.,[20] and his colleagues developed a stages-of-change model called the transtheoretical model. Here are the five stages:

1. Precontemplation
2. Contemplation
3. Preparation
4. Action
5. Maintenance

Let's take them in order. *Precontemplation* is when you don't think you have a problem. Someone *else* may think you have a problem, but *you* don't. This is a height of denial. I'm guessing you are beyond this stage, or you wouldn't be reading this book right now.

Contemplation is when you begin to consider that you have a problem, but your are not yet convinced.

Once your emotions are aroused (you're feeling triggered with fear, anger or guilt, etc.), you're probably moving into the next stage. *Preparation* is the stage when you fully acknowledge you have a problem. You see it; you can talk about it; and you understand what needs to be done about it.

Action (stage four) is the stage where change actually occurs. You begin behaving differently. Not only do you see the problem as your own and know what needs to be done about it, you are ready to do the deeds.

You make changes. You check off some goals.

You are nailing it! Cue the applause!

Well, maybe not just yet.

There is one more stage, and if you think you are done before you get there, it's a big problem. Have you ever gone on a diet and lost 5-10 lbs, patted yourself on the back, and thought *I'm done* only to find yourself gaining it all back? Most of us have, and I'm here with the sad news that there more work to do.

The fifth stage is *maintenance*. This is where you have made change, and you are working super hard to stay on track.

This is where most of us fall down. We pat ourselves on the back and call it good when the job isn't finished. (Self-talk here is: You've got to be kidding me, bitch! More work?!) I know. The thing is that old habits or patterns die hard. If you let down your guard, that shit sneaks back in and takes you to what is familiar. In maintenance, you have to be ready for the challenges of boredom and uncertainty. The more prepared you are for what comes your way, the more successful you will be at maintaining change.

The most important thing to keep in mind, though, is that in these stages of change, there is no failure. No failure? How can this be? Well, each time something does not go according to plan, you learn. You go back to a previous stage, and you incorporate the learning to better prepare you for future challenges. You see? Each mis-step makes you stronger if you allow it.

Dispense with the self-pity and get on with figuring out where things went awry. Move right on along.

· *GETTING THERE* ·

Behavior change starts with a naked level of honesty, no matter how embarrassing. You have to be willing to admit with brutality why your relationship issues are a problem, what they have done to you and your life, what power the issues have over you, and what they have cost you. This is not a time to lie to yourself—that is, telling yourself the change is temporary or will be easy. It is not a time to talk about changing a little. It is a time to acknowledge there will be pain and sacrifice. But it is also a time for you to look at the benefits and rewards of change.

What stage of change best describes you?

When you think about the things that keep you going back to a toxic relationship—those ugly realities you'd like to forget; the difficult conversations that would be easier to avoid—what pops into your mind? Get your journal. Write down the problem thoughts, feelings, and behaviors that you need to change in order to be ultimately successful in changing your behavior in the relationship.

SHIT JUST GOT REAL

Here is where things get tedious, but don't skip over this part. The devil is in the details.

If you are in the contemplation stage, you will need to go back to your journal, talk with friends, and find more evidence to convince yourself that you have a problem. No one wants to hear that your ex has a problem. We are focused on *you* right now.

Be a detective. Do the research. Watch emotionally evocative movies. Stir your own pot. See if you can move the needle.

Make a comprehensive list of the advantages and disadvantages of the relationship. Keep the list running. What is it looking like? Are you being honest?

What comes next is for those people who are in the preparation stage. These people admit that there is a problem, and that they own it.

The first step is defining the problem in detail. You need to make a list of things you want to change about your own behavior, relative to the toxic relationship. If you thought brutal honesty was fun, it gets better. Drilling down the details is crucial, although excruciating.

Get out that goddamned journal—again. Write down a list of all your behaviors that you believe must be changed in order for you to get out of this toxic relationship. It may also be helpful to phone a friend.

Next to each behavior you want to change, write down the specific things that need to change. For example, if you write that you need to stop trying to save the other person, you need to write down the specific behaviors—like calling to check in, calling family members to check in, spending too much time wondering about the other person. Get it?

Make a list of triggers that cue to the behavior. For example, maybe it is knowing that you will be alone on Saturday night. Maybe it is seeing your ex on social media. Maybe it is when you drink wine.

Once you have made the list, make a list of things you can do to combat the triggers. Get the fuck off social media. Make sure you are busy on Saturday night. Have a list of tools you have learned from previous chapters that work to soothe yourself (e.g., journaling, exercising, talking to a friend).

Make a list of barriers that will get in the way of change. In the example we've been using, a barrier might be fear of being alone. If you have not learned the ability to manage the fear of being alone, it will get in the way of your moving forward.

Now make a list of all the things you can do to manage the barriers. Some of the barriers may be the stories you have told yourself, the ones that hurt, like *You are weak. You can't. You won't.*

Fuck that. I would strongly recommend that you get professional counseling to help you here. Why would you not? And get someone who will kick your ass a little. You have friends to be nice. You pay someone to be tough.

Think about what you have learned. How have you grown from past mistakes?

Again, go back to your toolbox and think of strategies that have worked for you in the past. Plug these in: they're your treatment plan.

A detailed plan will include how to handle any shit that gets in your way of changing the behavior, what behaviors you will do instead of the one you are trying to change, and how you will cope when you want to go back to your old ways. Dig deep. Make a comprehensive list of resources you have and things you will need to line up to ensure your success. What friends should you bring in on your plan? What memes or coaching statements would you like to post around your home to provide encouragement? How about a change journal?

Once you have a detailed plan, you need to set a date to change, and be sure you are prepared with all that you will need. I want to emphasize at this point that you will have bumps in the road. It won't be perfect; but each time things don't go as you wished, you will learn something new that will be helpful in the next go-around. There are no failures, only learning. Make a commitment to giving up pity parties, guilt trips, and self-flagellation. Total wastes of time.

The piece that gets overlooked much of the time is having a reward system. When you succeed, do something nice for yourself. Make it healthy—not going on a food binge-fest. Really reward yourself for doing something healthy. This is about learning to be good to yourself. Celebrate the wins.

The final step is the long haul. It is maintenance. You will need to have a plan for how to stay on track, how to ensure that you don't lose your way and backslide. How can you keep up the momentum? How will your strategies change over time? How will your challenges change over time?

· GETTING THERE ·

Here are some additional recommendations for getting over a relationship addiction:

1. Get rid of all reminders of the ex. That means no contact with the ex; no photos; no memorabilia. These things function as triggers in your life and make it impossible to get your ex off your mind. Think about it. If you were trying to give up crack, would you keep it lying around? Would you have photos of it on the wall? Would you have photos of yourself on crack having an amazing time? I think not.

2. Do not to go places where you used to go with your ex, where you ex might be, or places that will remind you of your ex. This is just being smart. Why would you want to torture yourself?

3. For the love of life, stay off of social media.

4. In your toolbox, have a list of friends you can call—people who've promised to kick your ass if you try to return. Get some meditation apps like Calm, or Headspace: Meditation and Sleep. Bookmark some calming visualizations and meditations from YouTube. Exercise. Go to the library. Take a nature hike. Do what needs to be done to get your mind on something else. Sometimes it just takes fifteen minutes

of distraction for urges to pass. You *can* resist. I know you can, because you have enough brain function to read this book. Hang the list of tools where you can see it, like on the refrigerator.

5. Look ahead, identify, and prepare for things that will trip you up—like holidays, anniversaries, Saturday nights. What things do you need to put in place to prevent yourself from going back to the contaminated well?

6. Journal the shit out of your feelings. Get them out. Label them. Write guidance and advice to yourself. Interpret what your feelings mean, and deal with that. Maybe you feel alone. Deal with feeling alone on a deeper level, rather than just mindlessly doing what is familiar and unhealthy. If you are feeling lonely, call a friend or mindfully sit with it and notice how it changes over time. If your feeling is anxiety, maybe do a relaxation or visualization exercise from You-Tube or healthjourneys.com. Maybe you just need a distraction. Get up and do something else. Manage what you are feeling in a way that targets the feeling rather than just trying to escape.

7. Notice negative thoughts of *I can't*, self-judgments of *not good enough*, and the self-pity of *poor me*. Make yourself prove the thoughts. (Hint: You cannot prove them unless you are suffering from frontal-lobe brain dysfunction.) Remind yourself of choice. The one thing you can control is how you behave. You may *choose* not to stop yourself from an unhealthy choice, but it is not that you *cannot* stop yourself.

8. Argue your negative self-talk with MOMF counterstatements and affirmations:
   - Listening to you is what got me here. I'm fucking done.
   - Shut. The. Fuck. Up. Fucking liar.
   - Motherfucker, you are so much more than this.

   Pinterest has a lot of additional ideas to choose from.

9. As you wean off the toxic ex, it is a good time to look at what qualities were alluring to you. Was there something about your ex that is tied to an unhealthy childhood experience (e.g., was your ex similar to a parent or significant person in your life)? How was the toxic relationship related to your core beliefs (i.e., how did your ex treat you that confirmed negative core beliefs or what things did you tolerate because you felt you deserved them)? At this point, it is a great time to get into your head and do an interview with yourself. What drew you to your ex? What made you stay? Think about your core beliefs and self-talk. How does it all fit together?

10. Do not reach for the low-hanging fruit of jumping into another relationship. Stay the fuck off of Tinder. Sit with the pain for a while. Meditate on it. See that you *can* tolerate it.

11. Make a list of things you need to make peace with in moving forward. Write an unsent letter to your ex. Note the term *unsent*. Do *not* send the letter. You cannot *make* her see, understand, know. The letter is for you. Write a letter to your younger self. Get it all out. Then decide how you symbolically want to move on (e.g., bonfire).

12. Go back to chapter 3 and re-read survival strategies. Be good to yourself.

10

Peace Out

Liz was divorced from Leo a year ago, but she was still so angry. She accepted that he didn't want to be married to her and that he had a new life with his new girlfriend. She accepted he had joint custody of the kids. She accepted her life would never be the same.

And.

She.

Was.

Still.

Pissed.

Liz wasn't just pissed; she hated Leo. She still went off on him to friends. She stalked his social media, knew where he went on vacations, and followed what he was doing on the weekends. She guilted the kids about wanting to spend time with him. She complained it wasn't fair that he seemed to be having a great life while she still struggled financially.

She never got over the fact that Leo had left her for his new girlfriend. It wasn't that she thought he was some kind of prize as a husband, but the fact that he'd jilted her for that tawdry whore was unforgivable. She was never going to forget what he'd done to her. She would make him pay for the rest of his life, and hers too.

MOVING ON

It is one thing to *do* all the right things to recover from a breakup. It is another thing entirely to move on emotionally by putting the past to rest. Finding emotional peace around past hurt isn't about forgetting. It isn't about saying it doesn't matter. And it absolutely isn't saying that what happened in the past is okay. Finding emotional peace is about committing to oneself that it is time to move on, and putting forth the energy and effort necessary to make it happen.

Finding peace is about acknowledging what happened, acknowledging how much it hurt, and actively working to let go of the hurt by cutting ties with it. Perhaps nothing in this book will be as hard is finding peace, but it is doable.

IT'S A CHOICE

A lot of people struggle with finding peace. I get it. Finding peace can feel like you are giving someone a pass on bad behavior. But it isn't about that at all. Finding peace is giving yourself a pass on continued pain. It is cutting bait with past bullshit. It is giving yourself permission to move on from what happened because you deserve more. Finding peace is all about you, not at all about the person who hurt you.

So, how does one find peace? This is tricky, because no two people do it the same way. I will give you a rough idea of things to do, but in the end it has to be a good fit for you.

Finding peace starts with making a commitment to yourself

that you *want* to do it and *will* do it. You have a choice of whether to hang on to the past and let it devour you and define you, or to move on from the past. While someone may have hurt you, you are no longer a victim, because you have the choice of where things go from here—any time you're ready. This makes you a survivor.

Once you have made the choice, you accept that putting the past to rest is a journey. I cannot tell you when it will end; oftentimes, people don't even notice right away. One day, you may find yourself thinking "Oh, I think I am over it."

And it is completely understandable how this can happen, because the next step in finding peace is catching yourself spending time ruminating on the past. While you cannot control how you feel, you can control how much attention you spend thinking about past hurts and disappointments. When you notice your brain going back there, make the choice to focus on something else. By this time, I am guessing you know a thing or two about re-focusing your attention and stopping unhealthy thoughts. Now is the time to practice more of that. Choose to change your focus.

There may be times when you set aside time to heal from the past; but when it is not time you designated to do that, you should not be thinking about the past. Redirect your thoughts to your present. As crazy as it may sound, finding peace is about consistently and persistently redirecting your attention. The past has already taken up too much of your time. The more you catch yourself going there and redirect, the less you will find yourself going there.

· GETTING THERE ·

In order to find peace and move on, it is important to fully inventory what hurts you have experienced. What things have been done in your past relationship that caused you pain and may still cause you pain? Write them all down. Next to each one, rate where you think are in terms of moving on (from 0 = it hurts just as bad as when it first happened to 5 = I've moved on already).

Spend some time journaling about why you haven't been able to find peace around each of the things you have written down. Why are you hanging on? What has gotten in the way of your moving on? What do you think it would take for you to find peace? The answer to this last question cannot be what you want someone else to do or to give you. This would take control away from you. Right now, we are all about what you can do for yourself.

MEANING

This next part may be a touchy subject. It is about finding something useful or positive in something bad. (Perhaps you had to get up and pick the book up off the floor just now, after you hurled it with a profanity. I appreciate your willingness to give it a second look.)

Let me be clear. I am not saying you should be, or have to be, or even *can* be grateful that this happened to you. I am not saying that in order to heal, you have to see the bright side. But it helps.

Meaning is about the sense we make of events, and it is absolutely a matter of perspective. You can take any event, and no two people will see it the same. That is because we all filter information and experiences through our genetics, core beliefs, and life experiences. We all have unique perspectives, yet how we see the world will affect how we heal.

Making meaning is about understanding that all events have ripple effects, both good and bad. It depends on your perspective. It depends on what you see. Because we are programmed to see certain things, we may have to work harder to see the positives when bad things happen. That doesn't mean we are incapable of seeing them. It also doesn't mean they are not there. It just takes work.

Consider this: If I get cancer, which I have had despite avoiding many pleasures in order to be healthy, I can conclude that I am cursed. I can conclude that I am being punished. I can see myself as having no control at all and let myself go entirely. Or, on the other hand, I can conclude that bad things happen. Life isn't fair, but I have the opportunity to appreciate some of the real kindnesses people have shown me. I have the opportunity to reevaluate my life and focus on what is really important. The little shit just doesn't get under my skin as much, because I realize how fast it can all be taken away.

That is meaning. It is the conclusion I draw. It is the sense I make. People who are able to find some sort of useful meaning in shitty situations feel better. Think of it as the difference between people who use even bad things to grow, and people who get stuck in the muck.

Meaning-making isn't easy. For some people it can take a lot of effort, but it is worth it.

· GETTING THERE ·

Go back to your inventory and journaling. Force yourself to write about some useful things that have come about as a result of the breakup. Maybe it has made you realize who your true friends are or what is important to you. It surely is the opportunity to create a healthier relationship in the future. Maybe you can find some things to be grateful for, in spite of everything else that has hurt so badly. Even if you find only one positive thing, it is a start.

Keep an inventory of the useful. This exercise may take time.

Add to it as things come to light. You know, not everything is apparent right now. There are things you do not yet understand, but you will—in time.

SYMBOLISM

I like the idea of using a symbol to mark your commitment to finding peace and moving on. This part is highly idiosyncratic to you. That's what symbolism is all about, after all. It is choosing something symbolic that means something to you around finding peace. I once had a patient light fire to a bunch of very painful photos. As she watched the flames, she envisioned herself as a phoenix rising from the ashes—being re-born as a new person.

I have had other folks plant a tree or some kind of plant life that signifies growth and new life. Plants also give people something to tangibly nurture that symbolizes self-nurturing and growth. Still others have started support groups. Things could go in all kinds of directions, depending on how creative you want to be.

For some people, the symbol jumps right out. For others, the idea has to come to them after a while of letting the idea sink in. The point, however, is to symbolize to yourself that you are moving on, you are healing, and you are finding peace within yourself. It is symbolizing that you are making the choice to take control of your healing. It is symbolizing that you have the control.

· GETTING THERE ·

Spend some time contemplating what symbols feel right. You will feel it in your gut. It will make intuitive and intellectual sense. And remember, it is all about you, not the other person. A voodoo doll isn't a good symbol, because it is too focused on the person who hurt you. This is all about you and leaving that behind. Once you decide on a symbol, act on it. Envision the moving-on.

IN THE END . . .

Symbolizing the process is not meant to be an exclamation point at the end of the chapter. It is merely about creating an image and reinforcing the commitments you make to yourself. As I have said previously, grief and healing are journeys. I can't tell you when yours will end, but this is about choosing to begin.

11

Turning the Page

Keely felt like he'd been torn completely apart and then put back together again. He laughed because he felt like he'd known himself before the breakup. He had clear ideas of what he wanted, likes/dislikes, strengths/weaknesses, goals, and values. The breakup called all that into question. He'd done things he said he'd never do. He'd seen dark places he didn't know he had. He'd learned who his true friends were and what he was really made of. Sure, he'd been through hardships in the past, but this was different. This was life-changing.

Keely recognized that breaking up with his girlfriend forced him to reevaluate everything, and some things in his life weren't as wonderful as he'd portrayed. In fact, he didn't like his job. He didn't like the empty friendships he had. He didn't like chasing the next big technology release that would put him in debt for six months.

Keely was coming out of the breakup feeling confident in his decision-making, resilience, and life vision. What he wasn't sure of was how it was all going to fall into place. He wasn't exactly strong on patience and trust, but he also knew he'd have to dig deep to turn the page. In some respects, it felt like he was starting over, but he challenged the thought behind this feeling—

because he wasn't. He was starting from the place of having a really good sense of what was important. He was ready to find his true happiness.

ARE YOU READY TO MOVE ON?

This chapter is literally about moving on. I hope, by this point, you can begin to entertain the idea of turning the page on the breakup story, which means you are ready to start a new chapter on what you actually want in the future. This may be the acceptance stage of grief.

This idea can be delicate. I'm willing to bet you wanted to turn the page a long time ago, but it's not all about want. It is about want *and* ability *and* timing. You had to give yourself time to heal, to develop insight, to learn, and to develop the skills to move on in a healthy way.

Turning the page is accepting that the relationship is in the past and should be in the past. There may be sadness involved, and that is okay. What I am suggesting is that you need to approach this chapter intentionally. You have to honestly decide whether you are ready to move on in the sense of timing and skill, not just desire. If you try to turn the page too quickly, you may find yourself having to go back to reread past chapters or, worse yet, relive past memories.

You may dip your toe into turning the page and decide you need a bit longer to get here. You may read the chapter and not really take it all in—emotionally. You may need to hit the PAUSE button and read the chapter again to let it absorb. Or you may be all in.

If you think of your life as a book with many different chapters, this one is about turning the page on an old, painful chapter that has ended, and beginning a new one focused on enlightenment, empowerment, and vision for the future. All chapters are important. This one is a high note, but it is grounded in the idea that you grew from the low note.

This chapter is about your future. It is about happiness. Because you are reading this book, I know you've been struggling with happiness, and I know you will continue to struggle with it because you are human. Happiness isn't an end state. Happiness *is* the journey.

Newsflash, though . . . happiness is work. No one tells us that, but I will tell you that it is true. (Unclench your fist. I know it's not fair. But at least we can deal with it.)

I am not going to blow smoke up your ass with flowery admonitions to go out and be happy. I am not going to suggest everything will be just fine, now that you are in chapter 11. No, I like to ruin all the motivational talk with science—and yes, there is a science to happiness.

HAPPINESS

You've finally arrived, past all of the nasty grief work, to the other side: happiness. Now that you've gone through hell, this is a great time to reevaluate happiness. But what is happiness, anyway? It's not exactly an easy question to answer.

Happiness is something we all chase, and it is a respectable goal. The problem is that if you think happiness is being on top of the world at all times or being immune from life stress, you are in for one hell of a letdown. Our brains aren't wired to sustain constant feelings of elation. WTF?! So what is happiness, if it isn't constant glee?

This is a question that gets a lot of us in trouble, because we seem to be in a constant search for the next big high, kind of like Keely with technology purchases. A lot of people are confused about what happiness really is, and they start a chase of feeling high that leads nowhere.

Even more confusing is that happiness can be hard to define for the average person. I can't tell you the number of times I've asked folks "What makes you happy?" only to be confronted with blank faces.

I'm typically thinking *oh, fuck!* inside, because I know I've triggered an existential crisis by asking the question.

It's such a simple question, really, yet people feel dumbfounded. Sure, they might be able to throw out a nonchalant response if asked at a social gathering; but when really faced with the stark question of what makes them happy, people struggle. Sometimes it is because people have gotten so busy with work and families that they've lost sight of it. Sometimes it is because people have become disconnected with how they really feel. Sometimes it is because people have lost sight of what is really important in their lives. There are many explanations, but that's not unusual.

WHAT HAPPINESS IS NOT

Let's start with what happiness is not.

Happiness is not always having those excited butterflies we feel before going on a really cool vacation. I mean, the experience of a grand vacation is special. You won't feel that way getting up for work every morning. Your brain couldn't handle it.

Happiness is not being high on life every moment of the day. It is not going from pleasure-seeking experience to pleasure-seeking experience. Happiness is not a constant state of being giddy. Happiness is also not about putting on a happy face and thinking positive thoughts all the time. It is not about repeating affirmations and refusing to feel bad when you've had a shitty day. It isn't about avoiding negative feelings.

These days, I think ideas of happiness get twisted into suggestions to *just think happy thoughts*. That is absolutely not what I am talking about. Happiness is *not* about forcing yourself to think positively even when you are pissed, sad, or otherwise upset. That is what I call shoving emotions into your shit sack. When you shove all of your negative emotions into your shit sack, you become emotionally constipated. Then, one day, you just lose your shit everywhere.

You are meant to have a range of emotions, including the negative ones. That is life, and you are meant to feel them all because they all tell us things. For example, if you feel down every time you go to work, perhaps the feeling is telling you to think about a change. If you feel anxious every time you think about committing to a relationship, perhaps this is not the relationship for you. Perhaps it *is* the right relationship, but you have commitment issues. Who knows? The point is, you have feelings for a reason, and it is worth stopping, reflecting, and asking yourself what your feelings mean.

When you find yourself in a constant state of dissatisfaction or discontent, that is telling. Some persistent negative emotions might be genetic, but other parts are clearly situational, such as when you are in an abusive relationship or a toxic work environment. Again, self-awareness is necessary to figure out what discontent is about, in order to know how to fix it in an intentional way.

So it isn't healthy to be discontented all of the time, and this clearly isn't what happiness looks like. If happiness is also not smiling and being cheerful every moment, what is it?

WHAT IS HAPPINESS?

Consider two types of happiness.

One type of happiness is feeling happy in the moment, and the other is happiness as a general state of being day-to-day.

Perhaps the best analogy is weather. There is the general climate forecast, and then the daily weather. So, if it is summer in Michigan, I can expect the daily temperature to range in the 80s to 90s. It will typically be very warm to hot, but it won't be snowing. This is the climate. That being said, the sun won't shine every day. There will be cloudy days, rainy days. This is the daily weather.

The overall climate of an area is like mood. Mood is the more stable overall feeling or outlook. I can have a generally happy mood, meaning I'm generally in good spirits and feeling positive. The daily weather is *affect*. Affect is how you are feeling in that moment. So, I can be a generally happy person and still have sad times. I can also be a generally unhappy person and still have happy times.

The overall climate of happiness is consistent with a stable sense of being satisfied and content. There are moments or days when people will feel a range of other emotions, including joy, pleasure, fulfillment, and gratitude, disappointment, anger, or sadness. Generally happy people will feel negative emotions, but the negative emotions won't last indefinitely. When the negative emotion subsides, the happy person will go back to baseline satisfaction.

The weather analogy is important to understand, because it highlights some impossibilities. Happiness as constant elation is not possible. A better goal is happiness as a general climate, accepting some daily variations in the weather.

FINDING HAPPINESS

Luckily, there is a lot of research[21-2] on ways to improve our happiness both as a baseline and for a momentary boost. Notice that I am not saying "chase" our happiness or "control" our happiness. In the end, remember that I am talking about overall life satisfaction, not about being in a constant state of feeling *on top of the world.*

Notice I also did not say "buy your happiness." I will take this opportunity to point out that there is no consistent relationship between money and happiness, unless you are so poor that you have no money for food and shelter. Happiness is also not found in things that you buy. While this may lift your mood for a day or two, you will quickly feel that craving for another crack-like purchase. This is not happiness.

As I said in the beginning, I want you to think about happiness as a journey, not an end state. If you take this approach, you accept that what makes you happy will change across your lifespan. You also allow yourself the flexibility to explore and experiment with what makes you happy, knowing it is part of the process. It is all about self-discovery. There is no right or wrong. There is only knowledge.

HAPPINESS AND VALUES

I believe a helpful step in finding your happiness is to address values, which is another gargantuan topic. There is no way in the world I am going to be able to capture all the potential values you might have. You can do an Internet search to give you endless value suggestions. Here I will list a few common values to give you the idea:

Health
Family
Spirituality
Freedom
Service

Integrity

Hard Work

Values are qualities that you deem important in your life. You find them worthwhile, and perhaps they reflect your moral character. There are no "right" or "wrong" values. They are personal to you.

How in the world are values related to happiness? Well, my friend, many of us are able to identify our values, but we may find that our lives are out of sync with those values. This can be a deep source of unhappiness that sort of creeps up on people unwittingly. And it just happens. We have good intentions, but life gets busy. Shit happens, and voila! We find ourselves living a life separate from what we wanted.

For example, Tia values family above all else, but she spends very little time with family because she is working all the time. She works a lot because she wants to give her family financial security, and this means they will have the things in life they want. This creates a rift between Tia and her husband, and Tia is deeply unhappy. She is living a life out of sync with her values, and it isn't because she is making poor choices: it is a pattern she has fallen into, and she is not sure how to change it.

Consider Mathilde, who highly values integrity and honesty, but lives with Madelyn, who lies and cheats her way through life. Madelyn often asks Mathilde to "cover" for her. Mathilde feels dirty and unhappy, but she doesn't know how to stop, because things are too deeply twisted.

Living a life in sync with values increases happiness. Think of it as having a chiropractic adjustment. Before you go see the chiropractor, you are all kinked up and in pain. You get things popped back into place by the chiropractor, and you immediately feel free, loose, and pain-free. There is a flow . . . a sense of ease. When things get bunched up due to malalignment, we feel off-kilter and are even in pain.

· GETTING THERE ·

Take a moment to consider your values—what is deeply important to you. Rank these items. Now create a ranking of the values
based on how you are living your life. By this, I mean: If someone were to observe your life, how would they rank your values
based on how you are living? How well do the lists of what you
value and how you actually live your life match up? What things
are misaligned? What value conflicts are getting in the way of
your happiness?

Now, shift your attention back to happiness.

Ask yourself these questions:

What have you been telling yourself about happiness?

How have you been measuring happiness?

What have you been ignoring about happiness?

How have your relationship choices affected your happiness?

How will you need to change your ideas of happiness, now that
you are no longer in a relationship?

What things stand out that need to be addressed first?

If you want to know more about values clarification, check out
this great resource: www.actmindfully.com.au/upimages/2016
_Complete_Worksheets_for_Russ_Harris_ACT_Books.pdf

BOOSTING HAPPINESS

As I mentioned previously, positive psychology is getting a lot of attention in the literature. More and more researchers are looking at evidence-based ways by which people can improve their mood and feel happy more often.

Here are my recommendations for increasing happiness:

1. Have at least two or three real friends whom you can trust. As we get busy with life, it is too easy to let friendships slide and go by the wayside, particularly if you are a guy. We need time with people who are fun, who bring energy and ideas into our lives, and who care about our well-being. This isn't just about having people around; it is about having *the right kind of people* around. Surround yourself with positive people and a positive, healthy environment. Think of yourself as a seed. If you want to grow and flourish, you will need to plant yourself in healthy soil. If you surround yourself with negativity, it will be like vines that get a chokehold on healthy plants: they strangle the good. Even if you are a person who doesn't need to socialize much, it is still important to be around others. Our brains are just wired that way.

   If you are not able to name two or three friends you can trust, you are not alone. This is something I encounter regularly, along with the question "How do I make friends?" This is an embarrassing question for many adults. Luckily, there are things you can do. I tell people the best way to make friends is to pursue personal interests. If you have always wanted to take a cooking class, do that. You will meet others who also enjoy cooking. If you enjoy playing cards, look for card groups in your area. You can always do an

Internet search for Yahoo meetup groups. You plug in your ZIP code, and voila, you will get a list of people who meet in your area (or nearby) around a particular interest or hobby. I have met many people who have found this to be a great way to meet people. In the end, making friends involves risk and effort. It is worth it.

2. Do good for others. Being dedicated to a cause or larger community not only serves to create connections and socialization, but it is also food for the soul. You feel meaning and purpose taking shape in your life. It feels good, and it can take the focus off of you for a while. Plus, there is the added benefit of social comparison. When we see how others are struggling, it causes us to reflect on how we are better off. It just makes us feel a little more grateful, and it is a great way to incorporate some of those values you identified earlier in the chapter.

3. Be careful about exposure to toxins in the environment. I am talking here about social media, pop culture, and the news. It is important to remember that social media and pop culture are very manicured, meaning that they are presented to look better than reality. The news is saturated with negativity and scary things. It creates a lot of needless anxiety. Try an experiment: detox from daily news and politics. See how you feel. I'm willing to bet you will feel more energized. That isn't to say you shouldn't watch the news or keep up on politics. Rather, the point is to recognize how much it takes out of you. Be armed and ready to manage it. Otherwise, it just feels like constantly being hit with bad news.

4. Engage in daily practices of gratitude and intentionally searching for positives in the day. This can be a hard one on a shitty day when it feels like the rain cloud is constantly following you around, and you just want to kick the wall. Taking a moment to consciously consider what you're grateful

for can ground you in the reality that your life is so much more than this bad moment or bad day. Even when everything seems to be going to shit, there is often something to be thankful for. I have a friend who says "Every day above ground is a good day." That puts it all into perspective. Practicing gratitude can be everything from taking a moment, saying thank you, doing a kind deed, praying, or writing a thank-you note to someone who has made a difference. I don't know that it matters what you do, as much as it is about forcing your thoughts away from too much rumination on what is bad. Again, when things don't go well, you will feel bad. I am not saying you immediately MOMF into trying to cheer yourself up. What I am saying is that gratitude can be a reality check for how sorry we want to feel for ourselves.

5. Develop positive visualizations—those where you see positive things happening or you imagine what you would like to happen. See yourself feeling good, doing good. Force yourself to take time and consciously consider successes in your life. If you think about it, we encounter a lot that we get done in the day. Sometimes it isn't so easy, but we plow on, never taking time to reflect a mission accomplished. Celebrate your successes. I encourage you to write down a daily success or two. Giving it due attention and having a record of it does help you focus on what you have achieved.

6. Schedule some fun in your life. As ridiculous as that may seem, it is all too easy to let our calendars get filled up with garbage to-do lists and obligations. Be proactive. Block out time for fun. Schedule pleasurable events. There is real evidence that this is a true intervention for low mood.

7. My all-time favorite mood-elevator, anxiety-kicker, and stress-buster is exercise. There is a lot of evidence that exercise is as effective as medication in treating depressed mood, anxiety, and stress. If you don't have any of these things,

then it just helps you feel better. It is a distraction. It is an accomplishment. It improves your overall health. It is what I call a whole-body detox, getting rid of the stress hormones and creating that natural *high* from endorphins. Test me on this. Sometimes I just feel like shit. I don't want to exercise, but I force it. I always feel better afterwards.

8. It is hard to be happy while holding grudges. Happiness is also about letting things go. I don't talk much about forgiveness, because people react to the idea that when they have been wronged, the other person doesn't deserve forgiveness. It seems to imply that you are giving a waiver to someone. That is why I prefer the term *finding peace*. When I talk about finding peace, I am communicating that it is a waiver or dispensation that you give yourself. You choose to break the chains binding you to the past, and you say "I'm done with that. I am choosing to move on for myself. I don't want the ongoing torment of hanging on to the past. Doesn't matter what you do or say, or even if you have asked for forgiveness. I am moving on for me." Finding peace is related to happiness because it can feel like a weight has been lifted so you can feel more content and happy. You are burdened by the past. Identify what grudges you are clinging to and notice how they keep you trapped in the past—chained to negativity. I understand it isn't about flipping a switch and being over it. If it were that easy, you'd have done it by now. Maybe you are ready to commit to finding peace now, however. Maybe you are ready for counseling, to read a book, or to have a crucial conversation. Think about letting go.

9. A great technique for improving happiness is noticing your set point and working with it. For better or for worse, we are all born with a genetic set point for happiness. Some people

have a higher set point, which means it is much easier to be happy. Others, unfortunately, have a low set point and find it very hard to be happy, no matter what is going on around them. It is important to know your set point for happiness and to stick to a plan to improve it. It will take energy and effort; but the sooner you accept that, the more successful you will be. You can't change the set point, but you can improve your happiness level.

10. Once you know your set point, you're back to being aware of the core beliefs that emanate from your set point. You're aware of negative self-talk and calling yourself out on the bullshit. Recall that CBT is about identifying the negative things you are saying to yourself and arguing them. This is an extremely important concept, particularly for those who have a lower set point for happiness. It isn't that you can help your negative self-talk, but you can help what you do with it. Negative self-talk is like having a constant stream of negative comments being whispered into your ears. It colors all you see and absolutely shapes how you feel. CBT is about identifying the negativity in our thoughts, calling ourselves out when we are overreacting, just being a bitch, or jumping to negative conclusions. It is about arguing back. Use MOMF talk to spice it up. *Fuck that! The fuck stops here.*

11. Combine your CBT and MOMF talk with mindfulness. Catch yourself predicting the future or ruminating about the past. The sheer fact that you find yourself thinking a negative thought or feeling negatively doesn't mean things are bad. For example, when I wake up feeling impending doom due to my anxiety disorder, I don't call 911. I say to myself *Oh, my anxiety is high today. I will need to take special care of myself and work around that feeling.* Call out your inner motherfucker and remind her that life is about this moment.

There may not be another. It is about not missing a single thing. It is about looking around and being where you are while you are there. Have you ever looked at a photo of the outdoors and been struck by the amazing beauty of the blue sky and clouds or green grass? I have, and I've asked myself why I ever missed it in person. I force myself to go outside to look at what I am missing. It is all around us if we allow ourselves to just be there. There are funny moments, funny conversations, lessons to be learned. There are days we won't get back. Mindfulness is about using our energy for what faces us at that moment rather than exhausting our energy on what-ifs and maybes. Mindfulness is mostly about being present in our own lives, not being on autopilot. It helps to remind our inner motherfuckers to be present and STFU.

SUMMARY

So, what am I saying? That you should do all these things? No, that would be overwhelming. I am saying you should find what works for you, and there are many more ideas that I haven't mentioned. Perhaps you listen to a podcast that is uplifting. Maybe you pray. No one knows you better than you. Try different things, but never stop trying. Sin and Lyubomirsky[22] suggest a "shotgun approach," where people who use a variety of strategies on a regular basis instead of just one are likely to be more effective. You don't get too bored that way.

Again, finding happiness is a never-ending journey of discovery. It is about values. It is about avoiding pitfalls. It is about being conscientious in doing things that build happiness and avoiding things that degrade it. It is about daily cognitive and behavioral exercises. It is about practicing to be in the moment. It is about finding you.

· *GETTING THERE* ·

Write a happiness mission statement. While there will always be challenges to happiness, which are you willing to own? What are your aspirations? What things are you willing to do to make happiness a part of your overall success strategy? How will you measure your success at being happy?

Do a vision board that represents happiness. A vision board combines crafting, visualization, and motivation. Get a post board or bulletin board. Cut out pictures that inspire you. Add words. Add color. Add anything that lights your fire. Hang it up where you can see it. Remind yourself that you are on a mission.

Use these tools to guide you, but they are not written in stone. You are not written in stone.

RECOMMENDED READING

Harris, Russ, M.D. *The Happiness Trap*. Boston: Trumpeter, 2008.

12

So Long, Sucker

There is a quote by Martin Seligman, Ph.D., in *Authentic Happiness*[21] that I love: "You should take particular care with endings, for their color will forever tinge your memory of the entire relationship and your willingness to reenter it." To me, this means in order to have a good hello, you must have had a good good-bye. The meaning behind this is that it is hard to move on with life and relationships if you haven't adequately or completely closed the door on the past. If the door is still open, the past seeps in. In other words, we carry baggage. It is impossible for the past not to affect you, and it wouldn't be healthy anyway. We need to learn from the past so we don't repeat the same mistakes. However, we need to take care that we have resolved issues from the past so as not to poison our future with them.

If we allow the past to poison the present and the future, then the asshole wins. Don't let the asshole win.

My hope in writing *Getting to Good Riddance* is that I can assist people to have a good good-bye and to move on. That was the work of previous chapters, and the simple fact that you have worked through them doesn't mean you are done. Grief work is a journey, and there is no timetable. Sometimes you may even be surprised to think you are done, only to be triggered again. This is normal. Be careful of interpreting it as a setback. It's just a trigger.

Move on, motherfucker. There is no need to bring it up and review it all over again. Deal with the here. Deal with the now.

There is no single path through grief. The point, though, is to keep moving through it. In order to do that, it can be super-helpful to have a map or plan. Now that you have picked yourself up off the floor and started grief work, you will re-discover the energy you need to develop that map.

Some moments, you may be crying. Some moments, you may be laughing. Some moments, you may be doing both at once. I insist that without humor (even in the worst of circumstances), it can feel like there is little hope. Remind yourself that you will be okay, because you will.

Here are my ideas for moving forward.

Go back and review previous chapters. Summarize the main points you have learned from this entire experience. Ask yourself these questions:

- What messed-up core beliefs got me to this point? What do I need to look out for in the future?
- What negative self-talk kept me in a dark place? What works to keep me aware of it and to change it?
- What red flags did I miss, and why?
- What will be the pitfalls I have to look out for in the future? What things must I own that drive my behavior in certain ways?
- Where do I want to go from here? When I revisit the things I must have, must not have, or don't care about in a relationship, what stands out as most important?
- What remains the same for me, despite this whole experience?
- What have I rediscovered that perhaps was lost before?

- What I am I grateful for?
- What do I now know that makes me powerful in my own life?
- Where do I want to go from here?
- What other questions stand out for you?

Now, kiss the past good-bye: "So long, sucker!"

Perhaps this good-bye kiss will be metaphorical, symbolic, or even literal. Maybe you will burn photos or cards. Maybe you will get a new hairstyle or walk with a new spring in your step. You will turn the page in your head and say good-bye to the experience and the pain. You will say hello to the knowledge and the empowerment. You will say hello to the present and the future. You will say hello to the new path of getting what you want.

You can't be in a hurry. Just walk the path. Notice what it looks like and what it feels like. Be there. Take it in. The scenery has changed. Keep moving, motherfucker.

References

1. Beck, A. *Cognitive Therapy and the Emotional Disorders*. New York: International Universities Press, 1976.

2. Diener, E. "Positive Psychology: Past, Present, and Future." In *The Oxford Handbook of Positive Psychology* (S. Lopez and C. R. Snyder, eds.). New York: Oxford University Press, 2009.

3. Pinker, S. *The Language Instinct*. New York: W. Morrow, 1994.

4. Burton N. "Hell Yes: The 7 Best Reasons for Swearing." *Psychology Today Hide and Seek Blog,* February 2019.

5. Bergen, B. *What the F: What Swearing Reveals About Our Language, Our Brains, and Ourselves*. New York: Basic Books, 2016.

6. Jay, T. "The Utility and Ubiquity of Taboo Words." *Perspectives on Psychological Science* 4, no. 2 (2009): 153–61.

7. Wilkins, J., and A. J. Eisenbraun. "Humor Theories and the Physiological Benefits of Laughter." *Holistic Nursing Practice,* (2009): 349–54.

8. Zhao, J., H. Yin, G. Zhang, G. Li, B. Shang, C. Wang, and L. Chen. "A Meta-Analysis of Randomized Controlled Trials of Laughter and Humor Interventions on Depression, Anxiety, and Sleep Quality in Adults." *J Adv Nurs* doi:10.1111/jan.14000 (2019).

9. Savage, B. M., H. L. Lujan, R. R. Thipparthi, and S. E. DiCarlo. "Humor, Laughter, Learning, and Health! A Brief Review." *Adv Physio Educ* 41, no. 3 (2017): 341–47.

10. Eckleberry-Hunt, J. *Move on Motherf*cker: Live, Laugh & Let Sh*t Go*. Oakland, CA: New Harbinger, 2020.

11. Lesser, E. *Broken Open: How Difficult Times Can Help Us Grow*. New York: Villard, 2004.

12. Byrne, E. *Swearing Is Good for You*. New York: Norton, 2017.

13. Kubler-Ross, E. *On Death and Dying*. New York: Simon and Schuster, 1969.

14. Cooley, C. H. *Human Nature and the Social Order*. New York: Charles Scribner's Sons, 1902.

15. Dictionary.com (accessed 4/11/2020).

16. National Center for Domestic and Sexual Violence (www.ncdsv.org/, accessed 4/11/2020).

17. RobertJSternberg.com/love (accessed 4/4/2020).

18. Centers for Disease Control and Prevention. "Marriages and Divorces: Change in the Reporting of Marriage and Divorce Statistics." (www.cdc .gov/nchs/nvss/marriage-divorce.htm?CDC_AA_refVal=https%3A %2F%2Fwww.cdc.gov%2Fnchs%2Fmardiv.htm).

19. Erikson, Erik H. *Identity and the Life Cycle*. New York: International Universities Press, 1959.

20. Prochaska, J. O., C. C. DiClemente, and J. C. Norcross. "In Search of How People Change: Applications to the Addictive Behaviors." *American Psychologist* 47 (1992): 1102–14.

21. Seligman, M. E. P. "Learned Helplessness." *Annual Review of Medicine* 23, no. 1 (1972): 407–12. doi:10.1146/annurev.me.23.020172.002203.

22. Sin, N. L., and S. Lyubomirsky. "Enhancing Well-Being and Alleviating Depressive Symptoms with Positive Psychology Interventions: A Practice-Friendly Meta-Analysis." *J. Clin Psychol* 65, no. 5 (2009): 467-87.

Acknowledgements

I owe an incredible debt of gratitude to my mother for showing me what unconditional love feels like. I am also grateful for friends and family who accept and love me as I am—even when I am wildly inappropriate.

Thank you to every person who trusted me with stories of love and loss, especially K, who inspired me to write this book. Your honest feedback and encouragement were invaluable.

Thank you also to my magnificent agent, Tina Wainscott, who believes in me, encourages me, and kicks my ass a little when necessary.

Finally, thank you to the Turner team for all of your hard work in supporting and promoting *Getting to Good Riddance*.

ABOUT THE AUTHOR

Jodie Eckleberry-Hunt, Ph.D., A.B.P.P., is a board-certified health psychologist and executive coach with over 20 years of counseling experience. She is also a recovering people-pleaser, control freak, and worrier. With a healthy dose of science, compassion, humor, and a few cuss words, Jodie knows how to out-maneuver the inner critic inside all of us.